W9-BUI-172

WITHDRAWN
No longer the property of the
Boston Public Library.
Sale of this material benefits the Library

BEHIND PUTIN'S CURTAIN

BEHIND PUTIN'S CURTAIN

Friendships and Misadventures Inside Russia

STEPHAN ORTH

TRANSLATION BY **JAMIE MCINTOSH**

GREYSTONE BOOKS
Vancouver/Berkeley

Copyright © 2019 by Greystone Books
Translation © 2019 by Jamie McIntosh
Originally published in German under the title *Couchsurfing in Russland:
Wie ich fast zum Putin-Versteher wurde* by Stephan Orth © 2017 Piper Verlag
GmbH, München/Berlin

19 20 21 22 23   5 4 3 2 1

All rights reserved. No part of this book may be reproduced, stored in a
retrieval system or transmitted, in any form or by any means, without the
prior written consent of the publisher or a license from The Canadian
Copyright Licensing Agency (Access Copyright). For a copyright license,
visit accesscopyright.ca or call toll free to 1-800-893-5777.

Greystone Books Ltd.
greystonebooks.com

Cataloguing data available from Library and Archives Canada
ISBN 978-1-77164-367-2 (pbk.)
ISBN 978-1-77164-368-9 (epub)

Copy editing by Paula Ayer
Proofreading by Alison Strobel
Cover and text design by Nayeli Jimenez
Cover photograph by Gulliver Theis
Photo credits: © Stephan Orth, except for the photos on pages 40, 48,
52, 56, and photo insert pages 1, 2 bottom, 3 top, 4, 5, 6, 7, 8, 9, and 16:
© Gulliver Theis
Map by Birgit Kohlhaas and Marlise Kunkel

Printed and bound in Canada on ancient-forest-friendly paper by Friesens

Every attempt has been made to trace ownership of copyrighted material.
Information that will allow the publisher to rectify any credit or reference
is welcome.

Greystone Books gratefully acknowledges the Musqueam, Squamish, and
Tsleil-Waututh peoples on whose land our office is located.

Greystone Books thanks the Canada Council for the Arts, the British
Columbia Arts Council, the Province of British Columbia through the
Book Publishing Tax Credit, and the Government of Canada for support-
ing our publishing activities.

Canada

CONTENTS

"Surprising."

EDWARD SNOWDEN, on being asked to sum up
his impressions of Russia in a word

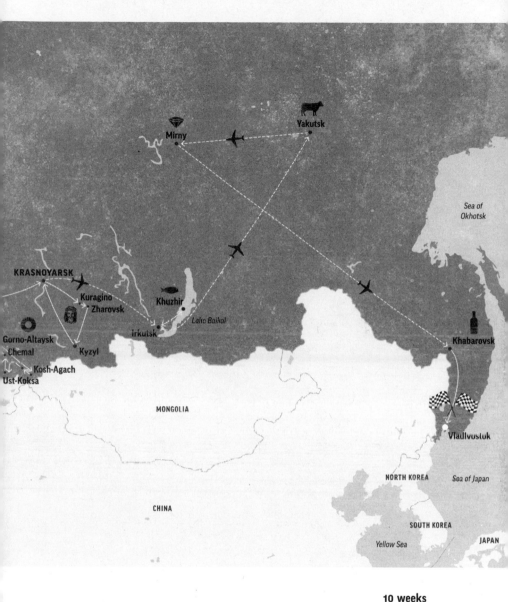

MONGOLIA

CHINA

NORTH KOREA

SOUTH KOREA

JAPAN

Sea of Okhotsk

Sea of Japan

Yellow Sea

Lake Baikal

KRASNOYARSK
Kuragino
Zharovsk
Khuzhir
Irkutsk
Mirny
Yakutsk
Khabarovsk
Vladivostok
Gorno-Altaysk
Chemal
Kyzyl
Kosh-Agach
Ust-Koksa

10 weeks
24 hosts
Total mileage 13,411 (21,583 km)
BY PLANE: 7,094 (11,416 km)
BY BUS/CAR: 3,870 (6,229 km)
BY TRAIN: 2,422 (3,898 km)
ON HORSEBACK: 25 (40 km)

★

ARRIVED

WE ARE STANDING at the edge of a crater; behind the barrier is an abyss 1,722 feet deep. "Welcome to the asshole of the world!" shouts the director of the Department of Youth and Culture. She holds her cell phone high to snap a few selfies of our small group. Smile. Click. Victory signs. Click. Hands in the air. "Closer together!" Click. "Now, everyone look goofy!" Click, click, click. Like kids at Disneyland or in Red Square.

The air smells of sulfur and burnt wood; the evening sun hangs low in the sky, bathing the dusty haze in red light. Romantic sunset, apocalypse-style. On the railings of the viewing platform there are love locks with the names of sweethearts: Yuliya and Sasha; Zhenya and Sveta; Vyacheslav and Mariya. Eternal unions sealed at the gates of Hell; lovers' vows at the most absurd tourist attraction in the world.

I don't know the people with whom I am being photographed. They have only just picked me up at a tiny airport where there were more helicopters than airplanes and more junk planes than functioning ones.

They came as three: the cultural attaché, the business relations consultant, and the student. So far we haven't managed to start a conversation; on the drive from the airport, the music was too loud. In the Lada Priora with *Street Hunters* emblazoned on the rear windshield, the seats vibrated. The student's driving style—he liked to take both hands off the steering wheel at seventy-five miles per hour to wave his arms around to the music—marked him out as someone who already at twenty didn't expect a lot from this life.

Where the hell am I?

The answer from Wikipedia: Mirny, Sakha Republic, in the far east of Russia, 37,188 inhabitants according to the 2010 census. Mayor Sergei Basyrov, postal code 678170–678175 and 678179.

The answer from Google Maps: ringed by Chernyshevsky, Almazny, Tas-Yuryakh, Chamcha, Lensk, Suntar, Sheya, Malykay, Nyurba, Verkhnevilyuysk, Nakanno, Olyokminsk, and Morkoka. It would be misleading to call these "neighboring towns," however, as they are spread out within a radius of 250 miles from Mirny.

The travel guide doesn't mention it. Even for *Lonely Planet* Mirny is a bit *too* lonely.

And my own answer? I'm exactly where I want to be. Anyone can take selfies in front of Big Ben, and why visit the Taj Mahal when there are already umpteen million photos of it? I've seen enough beauty in my travels that I'm ready for the other extreme. I don't mean the ugliness of a cockroach on the kitchen floor or old car tires in a roadside ditch. I'm talking about anti-aesthetics on a scale that makes you faint. Travel as a horror film or post-apocalyptic thriller: *Mad Max*, not *La La Land*. Ugliness with a wow factor; ugliness with a past. It's only the median that's boring; the extreme ends of the aesthetic scale are where things get interesting.

The "asshole of the world," as the locals call it, is a masterpiece of engineering. It took decades of work and clever structural calculations. It's the second-largest excavation of its type in the world. And it has hidden treasures. So far, sounds like a World Heritage candidate. However, the open mine at Mirny is no feast for the eyes. For decades, diamonds were extracted here, a few ounces of precious stones per ton of dirt. Glittering riches are still hidden somewhere in the morass. Slopes of gray dirt lead downward; a couple of rusty pipes are all that remain of the conveyor system. Beyond the rim on the opposite side of the crater, the eight-story apartment blocks of Mirny look like a Lego landscape.

In 2004, Alrosa, Russia's giant mining company, closed the Mir mine—the name means "peace"—for the simple reason that if they had continued excavating, the bottomless pit would have devoured buildings in the city. Now the diamond prospectors have to work underground.

"Do you get many tourists here?" I ask the cultural attaché.

"Ha ha, no, actually, just the locals," she answers. "That's why all three of us came to meet you; it was something special." But recently an Italian filmmaker had visited, wanting to shoot a movie here next year. "I'm going to casting tomorrow; you can come along. But first of all, a tour of the city."

In its best years, Mir was the most profitable diamond mine in the world. The biggest diamond that was ever found here weighed 342.5 carats. It is lemon yellow, as big as a cocktail tomato, and worth a number of million dollars. A sensational find deserves a sensational name, so they called the diamond "The 26th Congress of the Communist Party of the Soviet

3

Union." The "60th Anniversary of Komsomol" (200.7 carats) was also blasted here. Not, however, the "70th Anniversary of Victory in the Great Patriotic War" diamond (76.07 carats), which comes from the Yubileynaya mine, further to the north.

"Got your seat belt on?" asks the student, then off we race, slaloming over the dirt track toward town. Past a hillock with massive scrapped excavators and the inscription Mir 1957–2004. The Lada bounces over potholes, tires scream, and the student's arms dance to the beat. The two women from the municipal administration sing along to one of Elbrus Dzhanmirzoev's songs at the tops of their voices: *I'm a brodyaga, a tramp with no money, but still I'm going to marry the prettiest girl.*

After being on the road for a couple of weeks I've become used to being warmly greeted, but I have never experienced such a reception committee. Because of the musical accompaniment, the city tour lacks a bit of detail; it consists of the two women in the back seat yelling out the local attractions. "Main road, Lenin Street! Downtown! School! Library! Church! Fire Department! War Memorial! Stalin bust!"

Bleak concrete skyscrapers, many fairly new, and long, two-story wooden buildings from earlier years line the streets. There are no ground-floor entrances—all the houses are built

4

on stilts because of the permafrost. Without these platforms the ground would melt in the eastern Siberian winters from the heating in the dwellings. "You should come again in January, then it's minus forty, sometimes even minus fifty!" shouts the business relations consultant.

We get out of the car briefly at Stalin. The mustachioed dictator in dark-gray stone, wearing a buttoned-up uniform with a Soviet star on the lapel, looks proudly toward the city center. On Stalin's orders, after sanctions had catapulted western Russia into an economic crisis, the Sakha Republic was fervently probed for diamonds in the 1950s. That's the only reason there's a mine here, and the only reason there's a city here.

According to the inscription on the plinth, the larger-than-life bust was erected in 2005, on the sixtieth anniversary of the end of World War II. I express my surprise at finding a memorial to the bloody tyrant. "There was a referendum and many war veterans were for it. We're still a bit Communist here. Come on, we'll show you your room."

A short time later, the Lada with the disco sound system turns onto 40th Anniversary of October Street. This would make a good name for a diamond, too—they don't mean the month, but the revolution. We pull up at a wooden house with blue walls, on stilts, of course. The cultural attaché leads the way to the first floor, opening the lopsided door with the number 11 on it. "Normally this is accommodation for teachers working in Mirny," she says, handing me the keys. My room is heated to at least ninety-five degrees and has a sofa, a clothes rack, and a flat-screen TV. This will be my home for the next three days.

Truth No. 18:
I feel welcomed. Welcomed to the asshole of the world.

BUREAUCRACY

SIX WEEKS EARLIER

ANYONE INTERESTED IN checking out the profile of Genrich from Moscow on Couchsurfing.com should make sure they don't have any plans for the next couple of hours. At least as far as Genrich from Moscow is concerned.

He writes: "By sending me a request you openly state that you have read, understood and promise to follow the principles of common living explained in my profile."

In the upper right corner of the screen there is a black-and-white photo of a man sitting on the polished hood of a Jeep. He has hardly any hair on his head, but a full beard that the elderly Dostoyevsky would envy, and he scrutinizes the observer with serious eyes, deep, skeptical furrows in his brow. You could easily envisage his portrait on the bulletin board of a debt-collecting company with the heading *Employee of the Month*.

After the profile, twenty-seven screen pages await the reader. I learn that Genrich is thirty-one and is interested in a cappella singing, linguistics, cooking, orthodox theology, motorbikes, poetry, and dancing on the table. In the "favorite films" category he has listed *Easy Rider*, everything by Emir Kusturica, and *Die Deutsche Wochenschau* (German weekly review, a propaganda newsreel series from World War II). He speaks fluent English, French, Russian, German, Polish, and Ukrainian, and at the moment is learning Ancient Greek, Arabic, Georgian, and Latin.

The centerpiece of his profile is a complicated set of rules on how his guests should behave, spread over a number of Google documents with titles like "IMPORTANT MESSAGE FROM ME TO YOU," "I used to spend a lot of time in vain," and "When I host people in my home, I live with them." In case Google documents are not accessible in the reader's current location, the same documents can be obtained via a link to the Russian Yandex server, accompanied by a note: "And yes, it is accessible from mainland China."

From the reading matter I learn, among other things:

- that Genrich doesn't have ten dwarves cleaning up after guests and vacuuming the floor;
- that his apartment isn't a backpacker hostel;
- that he follows the principle of "rational egoism," which is why he will only invite people he finds interesting.

Half a page later he cites a sentence that he never wants to read in an email—it goes like this: "I am open-minded, easygoing, I like traveling and am looking forward to meeting new people." That sounds pretty reasonable, doesn't it? Not to Genrich. He thinks such self-portraits on a travel portal are trivial and vacuous. And because nowadays this sentence is probably just copied and pasted from another profile, it's just another way of saying, "I'm a lazy idiot."

Speaking of idiots: another link leads to a "checklist of couch requests" for the "extremely busy or extremely lazy," which raises one's hopes of speeding up the application process. It's a trap. A form appears on the screen with nine boxes that have to be ticked, which together form a sort of vow: "I will not send any copy/paste questions," "my decision to contact this person has a deeper reason that I will cover in my email and which I think will please the host," "I have studied the principles of common living explained in my host's profile, I agree to follow them during my stay, and I will mention in my request all points on which my idea of hospitality differs."

The accompanying link—as I have mentioned, a trap—leads to a seventy-nine-page screen document at WikiHow .com with thoughts and illustrations on topics like punctuality, hygiene, gifts for the host, length of stay, and toilet etiquette.

If you return to the form page and click "good to go!" without having ticked all nine boxes, a message appears by the empty box with the remark: "I would strongly suggest that you do not skip this part" accompanied by a black exclamation point inside a yellow circle. A tough nut, this Genrich. But I like tough nuts, so I write: "*Privyet*, dear backpacker hostel 'Genrich,' I am open-minded, easygoing, I like traveling and meeting new people. Have you got a couch for me?"

An equally tough nut: Russia. In the late summer of 2016, a journey there feels like visiting enemy territory. As if we'd gone back to the days when the saying was *Visit the Soviet Union before it visits you*. On the plane from Hamburg to Riga, I read a few articles that I had saved on my cell phone.

They discuss the possibility of war. The tone is more abrasive than it's been at any time since the collapse of the USSR twenty-five years ago. Wolfgang Ischinger, chairman of the

Munich Security Conference, Gernot Erler, the German government's commissioner for Russia, and Sergey Karaganov, the honorary chairman of the Council on Foreign and Defence Policy, all speak in interviews of a threatening escalation of the current situation, even to the extent of military conflict. During a stopover in the NATO outpost of Latvia, I look out of the plane window to see whether the first jet fighters are ready for takeoff, but am able to sound the all-clear.

On the flight onward, a blond Russian woman sits next to me showing her mother cell phone videos from one of the European Cup soccer games. The competition was still in progress. Russia had made an impression mostly because of the actions of its hooligans; they were more athletic and accurate than the elderly Sbornaya team on the field, who, as the last-placed in their group, were eliminated before the knockout phase. Obviously the team had been overlooked by the state doping program, another prickly topic these days.

I try to think about the last piece of good news that I can remember coming out of Russia. I can only come up with a performance of *Peter and the Wolf* that I saw as a seven-year old. In the end it turns out that the duck that the big bad wolf had eaten was still alive in the wolf's stomach, because he had swallowed it without chewing.

The majority of Russian stories in the German media are negative, and some of them overshoot the mark. For example, during the Ukrainian crisis in 2013, the German public broadcaster ARD was criticized in an internal review for airing "biased" reports. And just looking at the facts, hasn't the United States' foreign policy in the last twenty years caused more problems—from the Iraq War to Abu Ghraib—than Russia's? Why are there no sanctions imposed against the U.S.? The question is, of course, cynical, as you cannot weigh one crisis against another, but it's still worth giving thought.

People who want to learn something positive about the largest country in the world can fall back on the propaganda agency Sputnik. *Sputnik* was the name of the first satellite to orbit the Earth, in October 1957—a technological milestone that showed the world how advanced Russia had become. Nowadays, things are simpler and news is sent around the world to achieve the same aims.

Even more effective is the RT TV network, formerly known as Russia Today, until they came to the conclusion that it was easier to spin-doctor news without explicit clues about its source. With claims like "Telling the untold" and "Find out what the mainstream media is keeping silent about," Sputnik and RT feed those who feel they aren't being truthfully informed by conventional channels. From the perspective of an extraterrestrial, it would be very funny to note that many people knock the Western media as "liberal" or "corporate" propaganda while gleaning some of their information from Russian propaganda sources (sometimes without even realizing it).

In the West, people with opinions about Russia tend to fall into three categories. Those who no longer believe anything in the "Western media" about Russia because the press criticizes everything anyway. Those who read everything about Russia and are in the know. And those who no longer know what to believe about Russia. Most likely, the last group are a large majority.

There's no other country where the information situation is so confusing. That means there's no destination that needs visiting more urgently, at least for those like me who see travel not as a pursuit of fun but as a quest for insight. I realize that it's tricky to find such a thing as objective truth. People who consider themselves its guardians and owners are almost automatically populists, particularly in a country in which a newspaper called *Pravda*, Russian for "truth," has served as a propaganda tool for decades. But I still want to try to unearth at least a few certainties among the hundred thousand pieces of information that are sold as truths.

A B C
Alcohol • АЛКОГОЛЬ

The number one drug of the people and the main reason Russian men have an average life expectancy of 64.7 while women, statistically, live almost twelve years longer. In no other country in the world is there such a great difference between the sexes. Nevertheless, the situation is improving since the implementation of a nationwide ban on selling alcohol between 11:00 PM and 8:00 AM. In Novosibirsk, however, clever entrepreneurs have found ways around the law. Some of them "rent" high-proof alcohol, meaning that anyone returning an unopened bottle before 10:00 AM the next day would in theory be entitled to a full refund (of course, nobody ever returns a bottle). Others sell spectacularly overpriced key chains, with customers receiving a free bottle of vodka with purchase.

11

As preparation I took a number of Russian lessons and wrote some fifty emails asking for a place to crash.

My ten-week trip is an open-ended experiment. I want to spend time with normal people doing things that they normally do and not focus on politicians, activists, or intellectuals, as is the usual practice of journalists.

Each new encounter should add a new piece to the jigsaw puzzle. In the end I don't expect to have a complete picture with no pieces missing, but I hope at least to be able to see some sort of picture. I'll also be traveling to places where few other tourists venture, to become acquainted with the diversity of this country from west to east. I want to discover what's on young people's minds, what dreams they have. And I want to become a *Putinversteher*: someone who understands Putin, not in the sense of admiring him, but simply to comprehend the Putin phenomenon and its effect on people. Because understanding is never a bad thing.

The idea of this trip came to me on the morning of March 3, 2014. That was the day the German chancellor, Angela Merkel, said: "Putin is living in another world." I've been around a bit, but hadn't taken a trip to a foreign galaxy up to that point. It could be interesting. What makes Russia tick, what do Russians want, where is this baffling country heading? Finding out for yourself is always better than reading the news; a fool who travels is better than an armchair sage. So I quit my job at *Der Spiegel* and booked my ticket. Who knows, maybe in my search for normality, I'll stumble across something that evaded those on a quest for the sensational.

★

NOT AN ENEMY
OF ALCOHOL

COUCHSURFING WORKS LIKE this: after registering on the website by that name, you type in a destination you wish to visit. This leads to a page with a list of members offering a corner of a carpet, a living-room couch, an inflatable mattress, or, if you're really lucky, a whole room with a king-sized bed, a view of the sea, and a private beach (I was lucky in Australia). Host and guest introduce themselves in profiles. The friendlier your self-portrayal, the greater your chance of being accepted. According to rumors, being female and pretty also helps. Couchsurfing differs from Airbnb in that, one, it's mostly free of charge, and two, people try to present themselves—not just their bedrooms and kitchens—in the best light.

When I spent one long afternoon studying profiles of hosts in Moscow (in the capital alone there are more than a hundred thousand of them), I couldn't help thinking of *Herzblatt*, the German version of the TV matchmaking show *The Dating*

Game. At the end of each episode, an offscreen voice sums up the attributes of the show's candidates, followed by the question: "Who will be *your* match?" The format would perfectly fit the process of sorting through couchsurfing profiles.

Who will be *your* host?

Will it be Anastasia, twenty-four, who speaks fluent Lingala, who in "rare circumstances and on special occasions is not an enemy of alcohol," who can't sit still for long although she likes yoga, and who poses in her profile photo in a full-length, shocking-red dress next to a predatory cat on a side table?

Or is it Nastya, twenty-five, who loves esoteric literature and comics, who says of herself, "I am Love. Our World is Love. The World is One," and who, instead of a photo of herself, has one of a tiny dog next to a teacup with a cartoon duck on it?

Or Alexander, twenty-seven, with plenty of muscles and no hair, who describes himself as a "scientist, writer, and alcoholic," submits a photo of himself with a trumpet in some sort of laboratory, and lists his interests as "literature, science, alcohol, and sex"?

Or Olya, twenty-four, who likes Manowar and Britney Spears, works for a fashion magazine, has a "very cute cat called Adolf," and as a joint activity suggests "watching ballet and drinking vodka"? (In her photo she is wearing a white face mask, with her lips forming a kiss.)

Or Vadim, twenty-nine, who likes to discuss "all kinds of topics with intelligent people," knows all about martial arts, and can teach guests how to use Russian saunas? (The accompanying photo: a serious-looking guy next to an H.R. Giger–style alien sculpture made of bits of metal).

Or Natalya, thirty-eight, sitting on a quad bike in a black bikini, who is unemployed at the moment, prefers men as guests, is "cheerful, active, positive, and adventurous," and enjoys cooking borscht?

Or Alina, twenty-eight, who has a "small zoo" at home consisting of a cat, a dog, a rat, an Australian turtle, and a bird that all get along very well, and whose declared motto is: "Just do it, you can regret it later." (In her profile photo she is posing with two camels. Hopefully they are not part of her small zoo.)

Or is it Genrich, thirty-one, who speaks six languages and torments potential guests with more than a hundred pages of instructions on how to behave?

His reply arrives exactly three minutes after I write to him: "You have a keen sense of humor, that can be safely stated. I would indeed be glad and feel honored to host you on the dates specified."

Apart from this message his email contains two screen pages with precise travel information, a request for my exact ETA, and a total of fourteen links leading to maps and subway timetables. "I'd be pleased to answer any relevant questions," he writes, adding, "if they happen to arise after you have checked all the available sources."

OK, I get it: no further questions.

Truth No. 1:
Behind a craggy facade there is sometimes unexpected warmth.

A COUPLE OF days later I land at Sheremetyevo International Airport. Its unique feature is a flower vending machine that sells bouquets for 1,000, 1,500, or 2,000 rubles. The higher the price, the cuter the fluffy mouse or dog hiding among the blossoms. I quickly ditch the idea of pleasing Genrich with such a gift. Instead I've brought for him and other hosts some large packets of Lübeck marzipan.

15

I wait for my baggage nervously as I want to stick to my ETA. I take the bright-red, modern airport express to the city as instructed. I practice the Cyrillic alphabet by reading every sign on the way to Belorusskaya station: *Bileti. Kassa. Aeroekspress. Minimarket. Produkti. Avtoservis. Ekspress Servis. Gazprom. Rosneft. Makdonalds. Elektronika. Gastronom. Teatr. Metro.*

The startling effect of Moscow's subway stations on visitors may be due either to the lethal swinging doors at their entrances or to the magnificence of their platforms. Stalin's architects wanted to create opulence for all. People who lived like dogs within their own homes could at least stroll through underground palaces on their way to and from work. Today the subway stations are the most popular museum of Communism in the world, with more than seven million paying guests a day.

Belorusskaya is elaborately decorative, with stucco ceilings, chandeliers, and a larger-than-life statue of a soldier. Ceiling paintings show women harvesting crops, men clasping weapons, and children presenting their teacher bunches of flowers (without stuffed animals). In contrast, the majority of real

Russians in the subway car are immersed in their cell phones; wireless reception works even at two hundred feet below ground. Some have hushed conversations or stare into space. First impression: I haven't exactly dropped in on a laughter yoga class.

It's only three stops on the green line to Sokol, which has the same cathedral-like feeling as Belorusskaya, though with fewer paintings; in compensation, there are marble walls and polished floors of red and gray granite. For over a year now there have been no billboards disturbing the architectural treasures of the Moscow underworld. This, however, has nothing to do with aesthetic choices, but is rather because the advertising agency wasn't taking the agreed-upon payments to the city all that seriously.

A B C
Bouquets • БУКЕТЫ

Shops with the sign *Zweti24* are ubiquitous in Russian cities. They offer flowers around the clock. It's easier to buy a couple of fresh roses at 3:00 AM in Saint Petersburg than a bar of chocolate or a pack of cigarettes. The explanation often given for this 24-7 need for floral gifts is that men returning home drunk think they can avoid a death sentence by placing a bunch of flowers on the kitchen table. Demand is at its greatest on March 8, International Women's Day, and florists can charge almost whatever they wish.

Up at street level I orient myself with one of Genrich's fourteen maps and walk along Leningrad Street for some three hundred yards, thankful to be on foot rather than in a cab on account of the traffic jams. After an archway I turn right onto Peschanaya Street; at a German restaurant called Schwarzwald (Black Forest) I turn right again. After becoming acquainted with a couple of polite kids playing soccer in a courtyard, I find myself standing in front of a purple metal door that still smells of paint. How to gain entrance, Russian-style: press "K" for *kvartira* on the intercom, then punch in the apartment number (the keys resemble the ones in a telephone booth from the late '80s), wait for a peep tone (the peep resembles the sound in a video game from the late '80s), give the door a hefty shove, go through a second metal door, and I've made it.

My watch displays ETA plus two minutes as the groaning mini-elevator takes me to the eleventh floor. On reaching its destination it continues juddering heavily, as if not in favor of the sudden stop. Before reaching my host's hall I have to pass through two more metal doors.

"That's Moscow. A high-security prison," says Genrich by way of welcome. He's wearing a T-shirt with "Ask me, I'm local" on it and glasses that change from translucent to dark in bright light; a golden cross hangs from his neck. He has a ginger beard, which is roughly the same color as the *tapotchki* (slippers) he offers me. We speak English; my Russian is not yet good enough for longer conversations.

"I'm your first host? Well then: welcome to Russia!" He leads me through a corridor that is almost too narrow for me and my backpack and offers me a chair in the kitchen. "Unfortunately I'm awfully untypical of this country. I don't drink alcohol, have no bear meat in the freezer, and don't possess a balalaika. It's totally wrong, I'm sorry." He takes a couple of paper bags with cookies from a cupboard and spreads them out on the table.

The apartment, which he shares with a roommate, is some four hundred square feet and a prime example of efficient use of space. Built-in cupboards on every free wall, a washing machine fitted under the sink in the bathroom, and a couch in Genrich's room that can be converted to a bed. The guest bed is a squeaky blue inflatable mattress. After we inflate the mattress, my backpack has to be taken into the kitchen, as there is no floor space left for it. My favorite place is the balcony, with its great view: white skyscrapers, a building in Stalinist "gingerbread" style, an elaborate combination of Russian Baroque and Gothic styles, and the onion dome of an Orthodox church.

"Now, to the most important question," says Genrich. He strokes the cross hanging from his neck as if to emphasize the gravity of the moment.

"Tea or coffee?"

"Coffee," I reply. The answer seems to please him. He shakes my hand and says in an official voice: "Welcome to the club!"

He goes to one of his crammed-full cupboards, in which every object seems to have its rightful place, and fetches a pack of coffee beans. The coffee grinder makes such an infernal din that I almost fail to understand the next question.

"Stephan, what do you think about spices?"

"About what?"

"S-p-i-c-e-s!"

"I like them."

"Do you like hot-spicy? I don't mean blow-out-your-brains hot, just hot?"

"Yes."

19

He places a Middle-Eastern-looking, long-handled coffee-maker on the hot plate.

"Would you like a few spices in your coffee?"

"Which ones?"

"Cardamom, chili peppers, nutmeg, and ginger. I discovered the mixture myself; it's called 'kick in the morning.' Once you've tried it, you'll understand why."

"Then I can't say no."

"Yes, you can. You can always say no. It's my philosophy."

"My philosophy when I'm traveling is to say 'yes' as often as possible."

He pours the coffee into two Ikea mugs.

"Just be very careful with that in Russia. It could get you into trouble."

To prove his point, the first sip of "kick in the morning" blows out my brains. Genrich, on the other hand, seems to be immune to chili peppers and in no time at all has downed his mug. He then puts on his jacket. "I have to go now, an important appointment." He gives me the spare key to the apartment. "Make yourself at home!" The door closes noisily and I'm on my own.

★

LISTENING

A s soon as I regain the feeling in my tongue and my pulse is
back in the two-digit range, I leave the apartment and head
for the city. Sightseeing time. Moscow is the biggest construction site in Europe; new parks are springing up on every corner,
and a huge pile of rubles is flowing into a high-rise district
called "Moscow City." There are plans for pedestrian zones
as well as sidewalks, which have long been neglected in some
places, as Muscovites are not known for their love of walking.
(This, of course, evokes the old chicken-and-egg conundrum: is
it possible that Muscovites are not keen walkers because there
are no attractive paths?) The city mayor proclaimed a "Green
Summer"; green is also the color of the plastic tarps that mark
the construction sites of the city beautification program, and
there are plenty of them.

I go by metro as far as Kropotkinskaya, then by foot via
Balchug Island to the south bank of the Moskva River. Almost
exactly twenty-five years ago, the German band Scorpions
sang about following the Moskva to Gorky Park in their hit

song "Wind of Change." By "change" they meant a shift in orientation, an end of conflicts, Russia and the West growing together. Twenty-five years is a long time, and the dreams of those days seem a long way away now. I decide to conduct an experiment: What do you hear today when walking along the Moskva toward the park?

First of all, traffic noises, a cacophony of cars, and plenty of honking of horns.

The unoiled chain of a racing bike—there's a bike lane on the neatly concreted promenade hugging the river.

The click-clacking of high heels, the scuffle of men's loafers, and the regular beat of rubber-soled running shoes.

The rustling of wind in the trees lining the promenade and the running motor of a cab whose driver is nowhere to be seen.

The gushing water cascading beneath the 320-foot memorial to Czar Peter the Great, a drab colossus from the '90s—a time when a number of things went terribly wrong in Russia. The statue depicts a huge-masted ship, with the monumental monarch standing astride it holding a scroll.

This pricey work of art, made out of bronze and stainless steel, cost more than US$15 million and has the dubious honor of often appearing on lists of the ugliest memorials in the world. If poor Peter, who was a great aesthete and the most Europe-friendly of all czars, only knew. According to surveys the majority of Muscovites would like to melt it down, and sooner rather than later. Or else transport it to the dacha of whoever is responsible for its being here. Or send it in exile to Saint Petersburg (a proposal that was sharply dismissed in Saint Petersburg). The cascades beneath the ship were intended to give the impression of a ship moving through water, a point no one understood as the keel of the ship is way above the water.

I close my eyes and continue listening. The noise of an excavator, the chugging of an excursion boat—the Moskva84—the voices of passersby. One girl sings the chorus of the Titanic song, "My Heart Will Go On," as if wishing for the sinking of Peter's bronze hulk; her friend laughs. Up on the Crimean Bridge, the blaring of police sirens; below, the rasping of a road sweeper's brush on the asphalt.

A few yards further, a ventilation system in front of the park management building rattles like a faulty hairdryer. Inside, they have a lot to do at the moment, as a large proportion of Gorky Park is sealed off due to renovation work. Screeching excavators spread out sand for a beach volleyball court; two lawn mowers whine near the Golitsynsky Pond. A few beds further along, men with hoes and rakes hack away at the undergrowth to make space for new plants. One of the workers drags a wooden stick along a metal railing, each post making a different sound.

Sparrows tweet, pigeons coo, dogs bark, and kids wail. And there's also music. Dutch house beats droning from Pelman Cafe, American saxophone jazz from Chaynaya Vysota, and Noel Gallagher Britpop from the headphones of a passerby with a burlap tote bag proclaiming Open to the Future. Such a huge range of impressions picked up simply by listening. But there are too many different tones on the banks of the Moskva to discern which winds of change are actually blowing here.

"DID YOU SLEEP well?" asks Genrich the next morning in perfect German. Porridge is bubbling away in a pot while my host, with the dexterity of a professional chef, chops banana slices, all exactly the same thickness, into it. 23

"Is it true that all Germans swim naked?" he wants to know.

"Is it true that all Russians drink vodka for breakfast?" I retort. Genrich now switches to English; things are getting serious. "According to statistics, Russians are drinking less every year. In particular, vodka. Twenty years ago alcohol consumption was a *real* problem. But things have improved." His own history seems to bear this out. "In the olden days I liked drinking; I liked the smell and the taste. I loved Stroh 80 rum. But now my body has something against alcohol. The last time I went boozing with buddies I was sick for two days, real poisoning; I almost died. Since then I only use alcohol for cooking."

His most memorable experience in the military—one year in the infantry somewhere in the north, far away from Moscow—also had to do with alcohol. At a New Year's Eve party he went jogging to a store in his pajamas, in way-below-freezing temperatures, to replenish supplies with five bottles of vodka. A heroic mission, half an hour there and half an hour back at night in the freezing cold. His brave deed didn't get the praise it deserved: "The next day everyone was just going, 'Shit, which idiot went out to get even more vodka?'"

On top of the mound of porridge, brand name "Gerkules" (the Russians are not too keen on the letter *h*), Genrich piles banana slices, meringues, chocolate cookies, chocolate flakes, butter, a clump of frozen yogurt, and some lime. "Sadly I don't have any mint, what a pity," he apologizes as he serves up the best oatmeal breakfast in the history of civilization.

In the following days Genrich proves to be the ideal host, a witty conversationalist who has the gift of being able to switch from trivial to highbrow topics at a moment's notice. One minute he's lecturing about the linguistic construction of the progressive and regressive assimilation of *schwa* sounds; two minutes later he's moved on to the musical works of the

German thrash metal band Sodom. Sprinkled throughout is the odd reprimand or instruction reminiscent of the tone of his online profile: "As much as I appreciate your washing the dishes, permit me to say that the proper place for drying them is the draining rack above the sink and *not* the sideboard." He loves complicated sentence constructions and old-fashioned politeness. His polished English sometimes leaves the impression that we are in the middle a Charles Dickens novel and not in a two-room apartment in Moscow. Eventually he explains why his profile is so complicated. He simply had too many inquiries and he wanted to make sure that the people who contacted him were doing so for the "right" reasons and not just to save money.

FOR MOST PEOPLE, a vacation is the opposite of daily routine. Not for me; my vacation is in other people's everyday lives. When I'm with my hosts I visit their local pubs, look through photos of their last holiday, hear about the stressful day they've had at the office or the separation of their best friend. Within two or three days I get to know a piece of the life history of someone who was previously a stranger.

And then there are bookshelves. I'm a self-confessed book shelf voyeur, a practicing shelf analyst, a secret spine spy. I get a lot of fun out of creating spontaneous psychograms of people based on the reading material in their living rooms. It is, of course, appallingly unscientific. Who knows the reasons that individual books have landed there. But it is a lot of fun. In this respect Genrich leaves a highly educated impression; in his shelves you will find, on top of Jane Austen and Dostoyevsky, masses of travel guides, heavy scientific tomes on linguistics and biology, and books on ancient Greece.

I'm also a collector of stories, and so inquisitive about the next encounter that I've never experienced homesickness. Why should I? It's exciting not knowing who is waiting for you behind the next door. As Forrest Gump might have said: couchsurfing is like a box of chocolates; you never know what you're going to get.

For a coffee in the apartment of a Parisian student, I would gladly ignore the Eiffel Tower; an evening meal at home with a hippie family can be more rewarding than a five-course meal with a gourmet chef. While others get an adrenaline kick from bungee jumping off a bridge, I can sit on a public bus in a sinister suburb wondering whether I'm about to be greeted by a ritual murderer with a polished ax and a waiting acid bath. Such people do roam the internet, as one hears.

This funny old internet. The scope of the search functions on Couchsurfing.com is sometimes a little scary. Every day I log into a huge databank of people and filter them not only by locations but also by hobbies or keywords. How about a *World of Warcraft* gamer in Oslo? A tango dancer in Hong Kong? A nudist in Sydney? All are promptly served up from the website's people-menu, and the only thing standing between you and the next three-day friendship is a friendly email.

Of course, this form of tourism is far more demanding than traveling all-inclusive to Punta Cana or pottering around the Mediterranean on a cruise ship. Couchsurfing is not about a purchasable product, not about travel as a consumer good, where later you can ask yourself whether you had enough fun, photo ops, sunshine, and relaxation for your money.

My encounters are real; there's no stage management, just the mutual gift of time and curiosity. And for me that's more valuable than anything else.

★

ACHIEVEMENTS
OF THE NATIONAL
ECONOMY

MY SECOND OUTING in Moscow is to the VDNKh. Also known, slightly less cumbersomely, as the Exhibition of the Achievements of the National Economy.

In the old USSR days, the Communists put up exhibitions here—in over a hundred pavilions, with plenty of pomp and money—about the success of different countries of the Union and what specific branches of industry had achieved. Foreign delegations were shown around and "Heroes of Labor" from across the nation were celebrated with awards and money. Afterward they could return to their homes and tell of the grandeur of Moscow and of how all their drudgery had paid off.

After the fall of the Soviet Union the VDNKh also went into decline. The site was renamed the All-Russia Exhibition Center and capitalism entered the pavilions in the form of stores and market stalls. Consumer electronics, furs, honey, knitwear.

The park facilities were neglected; once-mighty architectural monuments became ruins. A somehow symbolic development in the turbulent '90s, when the whole country descended into chaos after the transition to a new system of government proved decidedly more complicated than optimists in the West had thought.

In 2014 the park became publicly owned and the mayor, Sergey Sobyanin, initiated a new strategy. Within days the market stalls were flattened; bulldozers and road rollers, builders and landscape gardeners were deployed to recreate the glory of bygone days. The majority of votes in an online poll were in favor of reinstating the old name of the site, and so once again it is called VDNKh. The result reflects the mood of the country: according to surveys the number of people regretting the breakup of the USSR has risen since 2013 and now stands at 56 percent.

On the way to the entrance stands the 350-foot-high "Monument to the Conquerors of Space"; depicting a launching rocket together with its exhaust plume, it is coated in titanium and glistens in the sun. Its pedestal consists of oversized relief scenes from the history of the cosmonauts. A small child in shorts and a polo shirt clambers around, first onto the paws of Laika, the first dog in space, and then moving on to the feet of Yuri Gagarin, the first man in space.

The park stretches across several hundred acres and is popular; there are plenty of families and couples wandering around. Renovations don't seem to have been completed; a couple of men in neon reflective vests are fitting bulbs to the lampposts using an aerial platform. Beneath them are trees, still wrapped in plastic, waiting to be planted.

Shooting galleries and a Wild Mouse roller coaster await customers, as do caterers at snack stands with names like Giovanni's Pizzas, Make My Day, and Noodle Mama. What the site map misleadingly terms "pavilions" are in fact temples. Temples to Communism, with pillar entrances, elaborate stucco decorations with imprinted Soviet stars, peasant sculptures, and a wide diversity of hammer and sickle symbols. At the entrances, posters advertise exhibitions on robots, Russian inventions, and modern art.

The most interesting structure is pretty much at the center of the site and is called the "Friendship of Peoples Fountain." Sixteen gilded female figures with serious expressions are standing in a circle around the fountain. Each one represents one of the former Soviet republics, dressed in national costume, with an object typical of their particular republic. The Baltic States, Ukraine, Armenia, Georgia, Kazakhstan, and so on. Even if today they no longer belong together, the sculptures form a harmonious ensemble (though anyone who argues that at last count it was only fifteen republics is of course right; number sixteen represents the Karelo-Finnish Soviet Socialist Republic, which only existed until 1956). Today's Russia is split into eight federal regions: Central Russia, Volga, South Russia,

29

North Caucasus, Northwest Russia, Ural, Siberia, and Far East Russia. They in turn consist of oblasts, regions, republics, and autonomous districts.

At the edge of the fountain of unity of Soviet republics, ice-cream-eating city dwellers sit dipping their feet in the cool water while their children play tag. The fountain is full of coins: ten kopecks, fifty kopecks, and one ruble. How does the legend go again? Throw a coin over your shoulder and you're sure to go back.

Truth No. 2:
Soviet nostalgia is trendy again.

★

THREE DAYS

NOBODY CAN GET more worked up about Communism than my next host in Moscow, Vladimir. After three nights I move to his apartment as I don't want to overstretch Genrich's hospitality. Vladimir is a burly guy with intelligent, if somewhat tired looking, blue eyes, and at sixty-three is roughly double the age of his predecessor. He has the unusual talent of being able to rant so flawlessly that during conversations you secretly wish to never return to positive topics. I quickly abandon counting how often he says "Oh, come on!" or "Fuck those bastards!" However, the words and sentences he slips in between swears testify to a keen mind; he's an original thinker who refuses to kowtow to the State or the media.

You'll wait a long time to hear him to say, "In the olden days, everything was better." The best time of his life was when the "fuckin' Commies" had just left the field, between 1991 and 2000. At that time he was hired by American foreign correspondents as an interpreter. The U.S. press sent their best people—the end of the Cold War was a major topic—and suddenly Vladimir was earning US$500 to $1,000 a day as an interpreter, sums that would have meant months of hard work in the Soviet Union days. Gold-rush fever.

We sit in his living room in the northwest of the city and drink Žatecký Gus out of cans. "Do you know what is to blame for the collapse of the Soviet Union?" asks Vladimir, fixing me through his rimless glasses. It doesn't matter whether he is speaking or silent; the hint of a smile always seems to be there—derisive, certainly, but not without a touch of bitterness. "Fucking TV pictures of German supermarkets." He takes a deep swig of beer, enjoying the tension created by his pause. "People didn't have enough to eat, mothers were having to queue for two hours a day to get food for their children. That's supposed to be a fucking superpower? At the end of the twentieth century? Ha, ha, ha! We had lost the race. Then there were suddenly pictures of German supermarkets on TV. Full shelves everywhere. Incredible!"

Vladimir gets up and shuffles off to the kitchen, which gives me the chance to inspect his book collection. Winston Churchill's *Second World War*, directly next to *Men are from Mars, Women are from Venus*; the Bible next to Victoria Beckham's autobiography. War, love, God, and pop. Four books, four worlds; a man of wide interests. In front of the DVD collection above the TV there is a framed photo of his ex-wife, topless on some beach at sunset. The most striking decorative object, however, is an olive-green helmet with the inscription *Ne ssy, prorvomsya!* which means something like, "Don't piss yourself, push forward."

32

Vladimir returns with dried fish, which he places on a paper napkin on the tablecloth. With deft movements of his hand he begins to skin the fish while talking about the Chechen wars.

"I was working there as interpreter for *Newsweek*, the *Los Angeles Times*, and the *Philadelphia Inquirer*. Looking back I wish I'd kept a journal or had a camera. It was unbelievable. They completely flattened Grozny. Like Stalingrad. Like Dresden."

He tears a large piece of filet from the dried fish and I follow suit. The consistency is like leather, but it's so salty that you quickly need that last sip of beer. With dishes like this, it's hardly surprising Russians drink so much.

"During the First Chechen War we could do what we liked; the Russians didn't give a shit about the media. In the Second Chechen War they were more cautious. Working there was very interesting. You experience suffering and horror, so many emotions." At one point he says he liked the job a lot; the next moment he claims he couldn't sleep the whole time. The press corps were accommodated in Nazran, the then capital of the neighboring Republic of Ingushetia, a three-hour drive from Grozny. "Luckily there was a sauna there that was open around the clock. I used to go there in the middle of the night, sweat a bit and drink some beer, then I could sleep."

He knew the Caucasus region beforehand; Vladimir grew up in Baku, in what is today Azerbaijan. His father was the head of a huge chemical company with four thousand employees and still not a rich man; only in a capitalist system does such a job mean a salary of millions. But still Vladimir was able to go to one of the best translator schools in Moscow. On his second attempt he managed to pass the entrance exams.

A B C
Commiebloc • ХРУЩЁВКА

English slang word for "Khruschoba" buildings: low-cost, concrete-paneled, five-story apartment blocks from the '60s and '70s that are found in many cities. At the time, head of state Nikita Khrushchev wanted a cheap solution to the lack of accommodation in Russia; aesthetics were secondary. Today many of the buildings are in need of repair and not a pretty sight. Thus the nickname "Khruschoba"— *truschoba* means "slum." Behind the front door, however, there can be surprises; often the apartments are considerably more comfortable and modern than you'd assume from their facade.

The sound of a key can be heard at the front door. Vladimir's roommate, a New Zealander named Nick who works as an English teacher, storms in. He seems fired up. "Such a shitty day!" he blusters. He had to teach "irrelevant bullshit" today as the stand-in for a sick colleague. "Sentences that start with 'you'd better...'—nobody speaks like that anymore!" Theatrically he tears apart two copied pages of a grammar book.

"Bastards!" agrees Vladimir. Exit New Zealander.

"Where were we? Oh yes, Chechnya. It is still a bloody key issue in Russian politics," says Vladimir. "Putin has poured a lot of money into the region, but now he doesn't have as much because of oil prices. It's a ticking time bomb about to explode. Ramzan Kadyrov, the leader, has a private army of twenty thousand men. They could suppress any rebellion. We will see. Nobody really knows what will happen."

He goes to the fridge to get another beer. I look on my cell phone, wondering whether there are any couchsurfing hosts in Chechnya. One hundred sixty-five are listed in the capital.

"The end of the Soviet times has proved that Russia is totally unpredictable," says Vladimir, opening the next can of beer. "I thought it would just go on for another couple of centuries or millennia. And then? A collapse within *three* days! Three days!"

What he means was the quashed attempt at a coup d'état in August of 1991. Communists and the KGB wanted to depose Mikhail Gorbachev, the then president, because they didn't approve of his democratic ideas, so they held him under house arrest at his dacha in Crimea. At the same time, supporters of the "State Committee on the State of Emergency" besieged the "White House," Russia's parliament building. The future first President of Russia, Boris Yeltsin, an anti-putschist, climbed onto a tank and gave a historic address to the people and military urging them not to associate themselves with the "irresponsible and adventurist" attempt. The putsch was thwarted; the collapse of the Soviet Union could no longer be held back.

"And in 1917? The February Revolution? That was also only a couple of days! The Russian Empire destroyed in the blink of an eye! Un-fucking-believable! Many Russians believe that now, one hundred years later, something is about to happen again. I, too, feel that we are standing on a precipice."

I ask him about the basis of his supposition. He tears off the last edible bit of the fish, takes a large gulp of beer, and says: "Eighty-six percent." This is Putin's approval rating in a recent survey. "Eighty-six percent of the people are crazy. Okay, most of them, maybe eighty percent, are plain stupid and uneducated. They would believe anything. But I'm more worried about the clever ones, the ones that have studied in the West. They now call themselves patriots and people like me traitors. *Come on!*"

"Why is Putin so popular?"

"Russians long to be a superpower again, as they were in the Soviet Union days. At the moment we are crap. But Putin and his press give the people the feeling that we are great, that others are scared of us. It's really incredible." He crumples the beer can and empties the fish bones into the garbage. "I have to hit the sack, I've got an early start tomorrow. Good night!" He trots off to his room, leaving me in the living room; a few sheets have already been placed on the couch for me.

I WRITE A few emails and spend about five minutes booking a one-way flight to Grozny on my cell phone. It's strange, actually, in these risk-averse times, that it is so easy to buy a ticket to a place most governments advise people to avoid. No *Are you sure?* query by the vendor, no I *have been informed of the risks* box to tick. It's easier to book a flight to Chechnya than it is to change your cell provider.

When the European media report on the region, it usually means no good. A couple of weeks previously, a bus full of foreign journalists and NGO members was ambushed in Chechnya and the passengers were beaten up. A few months before that, a branch of the human rights group Committee for the Prevention of Torture was the target of an arson attack and had to close its office in Grozny. A friend of a friend who had lived there told of a photographer working on a report that was critical of the government being burnt like a witch in the Middle Ages. Vladimir says he only knows what it was like there fifteen years ago and cannot gauge the situation today.

When, the next day, Murad* from Grozny replies in a brief email that I can stay at his place, I ask him by WhatsApp how dangerous he thinks my visit will be. His response? Four smileys crying with laughter. And a tip: "It would be good not to wear shorts. Have you got a suit?"

"I've got a black shirt."

"Okay. You're arriving at the end of Ramadan, it's the best time to be here."

Laughing smileys as a reply to a concerned query, from a stranger I only know from an internet profile. Right up to the moment of departure I am beset with doubts about whether this stage of my travels is a good idea.

What would a Russian do in my position? Maybe just stroke the snout of the dog at Revolution Square on the Moscow Metro. That's supposed to bring good luck. I pat cold metal; the dog's expression looks serious, but not without sympathy. Well then, nothing can go wrong now.

37

---

* Name changed

LIONS AND SKYSCRAPERS

THREE HOURS LATER I'm sitting on the plane. Most of the passengers are either women wearing headscarves or men with beards typical of the region—from ears to chin, but shaved above the upper lip. In the row in front of me, three girls are taking snapshots on their cell phones, holding their tickets aloft and flashing "V" signs. Their embroidered dresses and rings with precious stones look expensive; their facial features look more Asian than Russian. "We're studying English in Moscow and are now going home to our families," one of them explains. She just shrugs on being asked whether Grozny is dangerous, then gives me a few tips: "Always be polite. Don't touch women. And whatever you do, don't wear shorts."

From the plane window, Chechnya seems surprisingly green (what was I expecting? A desert? Bomb craters?). A melody from *Swan Lake* plays during the landing. "Ground temperature is thirty-two Celsius, with clear skies," says the stewardess. "Thank you for choosing UTair."

The airport building is a flat-roofed concrete block with portraits of Putin to the left and Akhmad Kadyrov, father of the incumbent President Ramzan Kadyrov, to the right. Both portraits are one story high. Beyond them you can make out the golden minarets of a mosque in the airport forecourt.

On the outer wall there are two quotations from the older Kadyrov, who was blown up by assassins in 2004. "My weapon is Truth, every army is powerless against it" is one; "Deeds are the only proof of patriotism" the other. Beneath them, brass statues of wild, snarling lions guard the exit. Welcome to Chechnya.

Murad messages me that he is still in a meeting; I should take a taxi to the mosque and he will meet me there. I don't need to ask which one he means. The "Heart of Chechnya" is the largest mosque in Russia, and in fact the taxi does stop in front of a heart. Opposite the parking lot a sculpture of large letters reading "I ♥ GROZNY" has been erected for souvenir photos.

I only know Grozny from the images I saw on TV during the war. Whole sections of the city that looked like Aleppo in Syria today; an apocalyptic atmosphere, with tanks among rubble and skeletons of houses.

Now I'm standing in front of a magnificent mosque with marble-coated walls. Not a speck of dust can be found on the polished stone floor in front; not a single leaf protrudes even a fraction of an inch from the precisely trimmed hedge. Just beyond, the skyscrapers of Grozny City tower above, the sight of them reminding me more of Abu Dhabi than a bomb site.

With billions of dollars from Moscow, the city was rebuilt after the war, with the planned Akhmat Tower as the new landmark. If you look at the plans for the proposed highest skyscraper in the country using a bit of imagination, it's impossible to ignore its similarity to a gigantic penis. In gratitude for the financial support for such prestigious building projects, Putin's Muslim governor, Kadyrov, and his black-uniformed militia, the *Kadyrovtsy,* ensure some degree of peace.

Peace, indeed. There's hardly a sound to be heard, hardly anyone to be seen—just a few faithful with prayer caps wandering around in the inner courtyard of the mosque. I can't quite grasp this place; I feel the looks directed at me. A foreigner with a backpack and a camera stands out. Tourists don't usually come here.

A silver Toyota sedan stops in front of me. The rear windows are tinted; two men with short black hair and light checked shirts get out. They look serious and approach me quickly.

"Stephan?" asks one of them.

"Murad?" I reply, and we shake hands. The second man is his brother, Ruslan. I wish them well for the end of Ramadan and then climb into the back seat.

For the tour of the city I sit behind the tinted windows as if I were a spy. "The main street used to be called Victory Avenue; now, leading up to the mosque, it's called 'Putin Prospect,' and after the mosque, 'Kadyrov Prospect,'" explains Murad. Here, too, everything is clean, everything looks new. "And now we are passing the Memorial to the Three Idiots!" He points to a statue of three Bolshevik soldiers. Chechens believe that anyone who fought for the Communists must have been an idiot, hence the statue's nickname.

Chechens don't have happy memories of the Soviet times, especially because toward the end of World War II, hundreds of thousands of their people were deported. Nevertheless, the parallel street is still named after Rosa Luxemburg. Restaurants, on the other hand, indicate a new breed of heroes: not far from "Hollywood1" you will find the "HalAl Pacino Café."

We stop and get out at a wasteland outside the city center. Here nothing is clean or renovated. Churned-up gray soil, rampant weeds, a couple of hollows in the ground, and the remains of walls. "This used to be a huge market," says Murad. "Over there you could buy weapons. During the last war the whole area was bombed twice. The children's hospital was also destroyed." He talks without any visible signs of emotion, like a museum guide describing a nineteenth-century landscape painting. This probably isn't the first time he's taken visitors to this site. "Some member of the Kadyrov clan will start building here soon for sure, it's a good location."

For our evening meal we share a sixteen-inch pizza Mexicana at Spontinni, a smart Italian fast-food restaurant on Putin Prospect: bright cushions on wooden benches, English sayings in chalk on the blackboard ("Eat fresh, stay fresh"), a Disney cartoon running on a screen. "I hate Russia," says Murad. "I mean the government, not the normal people."

Postwar Chechnya works like this: "Putin sends money, meaning we have to play by the rules. The local powers are ass-kissers, they couldn't care less what the people think, they are only interested in what Putin wants. Whoever says something positive about the president appears on TV and hopes to gain some sort of benefit from it."

Investments from Moscow are always coupled to some demand or other: "If you want to open a café or a shopping center, then it's okay. But a new factory? Impossible. We are supposed to remain dependent. All industry was totally eradicated by the war."

After a short scuffle about who will foot the bill, which I manage to win, we drive to Murad's house, just outside the center of town. An almost ten-foot brick wall with a heavy steel door protects an overgrown garden, in which he parks the car. He lives on a construction site: the ground floor, with three rooms, a huge bathroom, and a kitchen, is almost finished. The concrete staircase leads up to the attic, and here the floorboards and paneling are missing; planks and paint buckets are scattered around. "I have to earn a bit of money before I can carry on," explains Murad. He dreams of organizing trips for tourists one day in the future. Before that happens the security situation will have to improve and foreign offices will have to be convinced to change their travel warnings.

Maybe it would be advisable to prepare a revised version of the current "Visit Chechnya" brochure, which he handed me. In it, the deputy director of a tour organization called Tour Ex poses clenching a knife. The text beneath the photo states that whoever travels with him is "guaranteed a comfortable trip."

A collection of Chechen postcards, on the other hand, is more inviting. Among them are pictures of illuminated mosques at night, flowering meadows against a hill landscape, and historical watchtowers.

КОЛЛЕКТИВ

И ГОСТИ!

ХАВАЖ БАКАНАЕВ   МАДИНА

Заместитель директора ГУП «Тур-
Эис» : гарант вашего беззаботного
пребывания в Чеченской
Республике, опытный организатор
и надежный помощник.

Дипломатичн
объедила мн
знает о

THE NEXT MORNING we put on our best clothes, polish our shoes, and drive to Ingushetia. We're visiting relatives in the neighboring republic: Murad, his brother, their father (who dropped by the previous evening), and me. "You've chosen the best day of the year; today we celebrate the end of Ramadan," says Murad. He turns on the car stereo and we head down the highway toward the outskirts of Grozny listening to the songs of Scooter: "Mesmerized," "Metropolis," and "Psycho." Sterile music to match the sterile houses and sterile streets; everything clean, highly polished, and artificial. But something isn't quite right with this placidity; it feels like a *Truman Show* idyll, a Potemkinesque illusion. People here are frightened of their government; they haven't yet come to terms with the trauma of the last war, which only ended in 2009. I notice that disabled veterans are nowhere to be seen.

43

Chechnya is a unique experiment in radical reconciliation with the past: Can you simply pave over the traces of two wars? Can you slap new asphalt and a new city on top, put an authoritarian potentate in charge, and be done with it?

The First Chechen War, from 1994–96, was about independence from Russia; so was the second war, which started in 1999 and lasted ten years. It was an era of terror, with a death toll of more than 150,000 and the whole spectrum of war crimes and atrocities that people are capable of.

IN ALKHAN-YURT WE pass a crimson-red house with a Rolls Royce parked outside. "Dr. Bayev is entertaining some VIPS," explains Murad. "He is a doctor who during the war treated the wounded from both sides. A real hero. But his fame is down to one single operation: he amputated Shamil Basayev's right leg after he had stepped on a mine. He saved his life."

Basayev was like Russia's Bin Laden: the most wanted terrorist in the country. After the amputation he could no longer be an active assassin, which didn't hinder him from planning the taking of hostages at Moscow's Dubrovka Theater in 2002 and at a school in Beslan in 2004, as well as the assassination of Akhmad Kadyrov. The Russian government offered a bounty of US$9.5 million for Basayev, dead or alive; he was eventually assassinated by the FSB, Russia's security service.

Police with Kalashnikovs stand at many crossroads; at each entrance to the village, huge portraits of the rulers hang on archways above the street. The bearded elder Kadyrov, mostly pictured in a black-and-white pillbox hat and spotted tie, smiling like a wise shepherd. Or sometimes in a thinking pose, with his hand clutching his chin: "Hmm... which dissident's toes are we going to chop off today?" One particularly irritating poster shows a veiled woman and the ex-leader in two heart-shaped frames linked with the text *From Heart to Heart*. His son is presented either in military uniform with an array of medals on his lapel or dapper in a blue jacket with a red tie. And President Putin holds himself as you would expect: earnest, slightly looking down his nose, and emotionally neutral. A cult of leadership that we recognize from other autocratic regimes. "Before, there were even more images where you could see all three in one picture," says Murad. "But they quickly earned the nickname 'Father, Son and Holy Ghost.' Once people started making fun of them, many were taken down."

Ramzan Kadyrov is less sensitive about being a potential butt of jokes in his Instagram profile, which has more than two million followers. There he posts photos and videos of political gatherings, martial arts competitions, and children's birthday parties. Sometimes he can be seen posing with a rifle at a shooting range while bad-mouthing his enemies; other photos show him in more private settings, working out in a fitness center or holding a cute pet in his arms.

The most absurd publicity stunt so far is a video of him wrestling a crocodile, which is so heavily edited that it's not quite certain how heroic his triumph actually is. He has already posted more than eight thousand times, and his media team ensures that he is depicted as a strong leader with a soft heart. The number of emoticons in some of his posts seems less than statesmanlike, as does the fact that he comes across as an over-enthusiastic Chechen tourist, forever snapping selfies. But maybe his age is to blame. At forty, after ten years in office, he is still one of the youngest of his métier.

But the laid-back appearance is deceptive. Kadyrov, who once fought against the Russians before changing sides, is considered a ruthless despot and intimidates his people with the aid of his private army. Human rights activists accuse the government of kidnappings, contract killings, and rape, and in the prisons, torture methods from the Middle Ages are daily business. After the murder of a well-known opposition politician, Boris Nemtsov, a number of clues pointed to Kadyrov's inner circle, but of course he disclaims any connection.

In front of us is a white Hyundai suv with the letters KRA on the license plate. "That stands for 'Kadyrov Ramzan Akhmadovich' and it means that the driver is close to the ruling family," explains Murad.

We stop at a house with a large courtyard enclosed by a fence. In the kitchen a wooden table bends under the weight of countless delicacies. "A cousin," says Murad as a tall man approaches us. Chechens greet each other with a kind of half-hug with your forearm glancing off the other person's forearm, as if you both have wet hands. This custom also apparently applies to men greeting female friends and relatives, so already on the second day I have broken my airplane companion's rule of not touching women. The feast consists of chicken legs and filled pastries, small meatballs and vegetable soups, mountains of fruit, cookies and cakes, and bars of chocolate.

A relative called Timur, wearing a lilac hat and blue shirt, is enthusiastic about my home country. "The Germans have done more for us than the Saudis or the other Muslim countries," he says. He is referring to the Chechen refugees taken in by Germany. "We have a joke here. It would have been better if the Germans had won the Second World War—then we would all be driving Mercedes!" One of us laughs out loud.

As a farewell, all guests are traditionally given cotton handkerchiefs. That evening I receive quite a collection: bazaar goods wrapped in plastic with printed brand names like "Pier Karting," "FC Barcelona Pfoducto Oficial" or "Charles Jourdan Paris." I learn the Chechen word for thanks—*barkall*.

At the border to Ingushetia, Murad speaks of a massacre during the recent wars. "Civilians tried to flee by car. The Russians made them line up their cars here and then bombarded them. There were no survivors." And today? Clean asphalt and, as a border station, a brick house with a Putin poster and a couple of bored Russian soldiers guarding it.

In Ingushetia the landscape becomes greener, the roads worse, and there are no more portraits of leaders. We drive through hilly countryside that would resemble rural England were it not for the places of worship topped with crescent moons and industrial remains rusting away all over the place.

Suddenly Murad's father begins to swear. "He doesn't like my driving style, says I'm going too slowly," says the reviled son, who, in truth, is driving so fast that you can understand why he has installed a beeping alarm system under the roof to warn of approaching speed traps. I notice how he transforms in different situations: according to his passport, he is thirty-seven; when he laughs, he looks twenty-seven; but when he buckles after being scolded by his father, at most seventeen.

In the hometown of Murad's parents we make a longer stop. We meet his mother, sister, aunts, uncles, nephews, and nieces, then walk down the dusty main road to visit some friends.

Everywhere there are richly laid tables, smartly dressed people, and congratulations. At one door I'm greeted in fluent German by a woman; although she had studied the language at university, she had never before spoken to a real-life German. Three doors down, a little old lady with gold teeth says that I should simply stay in the village—she will soon find a beautiful

47

wife for me. In the adjacent garden, another Caucasian experience awaits. A friend of the family draws his Makarov pistol from a pocket and shoots in the air with live ammunition. Eight ear-piercing shots, until the magazine is empty.

"He's a policeman, he's allowed to do that," says Murad. The guy reloads and hands me the pistol. I shoot in the air once, then I hand the thing back to him. Sometimes I'm not so good at practical things; apparently I'm not holding the muzzle at exactly the right angle to the ground. The owner backs up and shouts at me: "Hey, be careful!"

Truth No. 3:
North Caucasian men are not as tough as they seem.

WE DROP MURAD'S dad at home and on the way back to Grozny that afternoon we visit probably the world's smallest capital. Magas, or "Sun City," has 2,500 inhabitants and consists of one main road with a palace, a replica of a watchtower, and a huge all-round memorial. This commemorates both the "Great Patriotic War," as they call the part of World War II where Russia was involved, and the deportation of the Ingushetian population between 1944 and 1957. Stalin accused the people of planning insurgency and cooperating with the German army. Within days he transported 450,000 Ingushetians and Chechens by train to northern Kazakhstan. In transit alone 10,000 died. Today there is still much debate about the accuracy of Stalin's accusations; what is undisputed, on the other hand, is the brutality experienced by the deportees. It's also clear that as a result of this history (but also due to conflicts dating back to the nineteenth century), the relationship between Russia and the North Caucasian republics is icy. "We are not southern Russians, we are North Caucasians!" Murad is very insistent about that.

THE NEXT DAY Murad almost loses his car while performing a U-turn on the main road beyond Grozny. A traffic policeman stops us, asks for our papers, and wants to know why the rear windows are tinted. In Chechnya this is only allowed for members of the ruling clan. The usual penalty: confiscation of the car. An ample sum of money can solve the problem, but the bureaucratic process can take weeks or months. Russian traffic police are notorious for their unscrupulous administrative practices. I admire how calm and assured Murad seems while talking to the officials, in spite of the odds.

After five minutes of discussions through the driver's window we are allowed to progress. "How did you manage that?" I ask Murad.

"I told him the car belongs to my father and comes from Ingushetia, where the rules about the windows don't apply. And I told him that I was just showing a tourist our country. At some point he just said: 'Okay, carry on.'"

Not far from Grozny we stop at the Haja Aymani Kadyrova Mosque in the town of Argun. It is a huge, new building next to a traffic circle, and it resembles a gold-striped UFO with

49

three minarets. A guard dressed in black who introduces himself as Harbi greets me in a friendly way. "I like Germany: the punctuality, the tidiness, the beautiful language." Among his friends he has even acquired the nickname "The German" as he is so tidy. While I'm in the inner room admiring a chandelier the size of a small car, I suddenly hear music coming from the entrance. A song that really has no place in a mosque—"Was wollen wir trinken, sieben Tage lang?" ("What shall we drink for seven days?"), a popular German drinking song—is flowing out of the speaker of Harbi's cell phone, obviously for my benefit. The good man probably has no idea what the song is about. There is a strict ban on alcohol in Chechnya. Of all the welcoming gestures I've received, this must be the most bizarre.

"Why is Moscow investing so much money in Chechnya?" I ask Murad once we're back home.

He mulls over the question while pouring black tea. "Such investments are saying: 'If we choose, we can destroy you. And if we choose, you can prosper.' Some people think that Putin wants to show other 'troublesome' regions that they are better off when they cooperate. Or he just wants to bribe us so that things remain quiet."

"Is it not also a kind of compensation for the war?"

"Everyone who lost a house received money. Almost everyone. It didn't work out for me, although my house was destroyed."

He then changes the subject. He doesn't seem to like talking about the war.

IN WILD
KAFKASUS

THE FIRST STOP before I continue on my travels is the bus terminal, the dustiest place in all of Grozny. Spectacularly dressed women with pricey handbags and high heels hurry past, ticket sellers shout out place names. Hurly-burly, bustle, and dirt. I feel as if I've just left a theme park only to land in the middle of a Turkish bazaar.

The second stop is two hours later, at the border to the Republic of Dagestan. You know you've crossed the border when the bus driver releases his seatbelt and accelerates even though the road surfaces are getting worse. A flat landscape, sunflower fields; the cars are smaller and older, the villages more unkempt. It's only a hundred miles from Grozny to Makhachkala, but those hundred miles lead to another world, which feels like it's a few decades in the past.

The Republic of Dagestan, with a population of three million, is infamous as a hotbed of terrorism, and its security situation is the most precarious in all of Russia. Were the situation different, the region would have the qualities to be a favorite destination for cultural tourists from around the world.

"In Dagestan there are more interesting traditions than in all the other republics together," claims Vladimir, a Muscovite journalist and tourist guide who has worked for a long time with the Russian *National Geographic* magazine. He wears angular glasses, behind which sparkle the alert eyes of a man with a mission who is so curious about the world and its stories that he has difficulty sitting still. His rosy face, hidden only below the chin by a patch of beard, and his bulky torso, covered by a "University of Vilnius" T-shirt, suggest that he's more interested in the pursuit of knowledge than in fitness studios. Vladimir moved to Makhachkala three years ago to write a book on crafts and cultural traditions.

We sit in a wood-paneled backroom of a restaurant called Khutorok—the name means "small settlement." It's dark and cozy like a hobbit hole and smells of beer and frying fat. There are sausages, dried meats, and a strong beef broth on the table. Additionally there is plenty of garlic sauce and a portion of *urbech*: a hugely tasty sweet paste made with lentils, wheat, almonds, and honey. "The best Caucasian specialty. In Moscow they sell *urbech* by the ton—and for much more money than here," says Vladimir. A photographer friend of mine had recommended that I meet Vladimir if I wanted to hear some quirky stories. "You should visit a few of the surrounding villages. Kubachi has the best goldsmiths, Balkhar the best potters. And if you want to see something a bit bizarre, go to Shukty—an oligarch wanted to donate to his village new houses for many millions of dollars, but it's unfinished. A crazy sight." With that, he's finished with the tourist tips for now. The proprietor brings a plateful of steaming *khinkali* dumplings filled with minced beef, and Vladimir changes the subject.

"The Caucasus region is a bit like Japan—very friendly on the surface." When he says *Caucasus*, it always sounds like *Kafkasus*. "But when you begin sniffing around for secrets, then you have to be careful. I get murder threats every three days." At the moment he's planning an article about an island in the Caspian Sea where real pirates live, and another one about poachers illegally catching sturgeon and making a fortune from fish and caviar. He once thought about covering the brothel scene in Grozny and the unofficial liquor stores, which have "an incredible selection and prices only 15 percent higher than in Moscow." However, he thought he wouldn't find any takers for the article.

53

I notice how much the danger of his job seems to appeal to him. The higher the risk, the better the story. Dangers, however, present themselves not only during investigations but also in everyday life. For non-journalists the greatest threat in North Caucasus is dying in a traffic accident. Or just after a traffic accident. "Last year in North Ossetia I was hit by a car. My hand was broken and bleeding heavily. The driver got out and said, 'I'm really sorry! I'll take you to the hospital, I'll give you money.'" Vladimir takes another piece of dried meat. "It's better when you dunk it in the broth," he explains, demonstrating how to do so. "So, I get into his car and he drives at breakneck speed out of the city. I found that strange and asked him where we were going. He said: 'Trust me, I'll take you to the hospital, but I left my glasses at home and I can hardly see a thing, which is why we're going to my place first and then I'll bring you to Emergency.' At that moment I realized he was probably on drugs and completely off the wall."

Vladimir is an excellent raconteur. His imitation of the driver's voice sends shivers down my spine. Also, I'm enjoying his mixture of adventure stories and culinary tips. "Take more of the dip. When I first came here I was cautious about it, but people here eat garlic by the bucketload, so it doesn't really matter."

He continues with his car story. "A little while later the guy starts threatening me. He wanted to kill me and bury me in the forest. I told him: 'I'm not just a normal guy, I'm a journalist from Moscow. They will look for me and find you.' And it actually worked; he dumped me on a dark road in the middle of nowhere and drove off. The sausages are good, aren't they?"

"Yep, not bad," I answer. "But the *urbech* beats everything. Why did the man want to kill you?"

"He was on drugs and was afraid he would end up in prison if he took me to the hospital. Someone in his state involved in an accident can get into real trouble with the police."

"How did you get out of the forest?"

"It was like a horror film. I was standing at the side of the road with blood dripping from my hand. A bus full of young, beautiful girls drove by and stopped and took me to the hospital. After two months my hand was okay. The strangest things happen here, it's the Wild West. A bit more garlic sauce?"

After eating Vladimir suggests we go dancing. So we take a cab downtown, the driver stopping in front of a nondescript nine-story office block on Imam Shamil Street. There are signs outside for the Beauty Spa Daisy and the Happy Sauna, but not for a dance club. A stairway leads to the basement, and only when the iron door opens do we hear music. "Only guests that the owner knows personally can get in," says Vladimir.

He trudges ahead into a gloomy room half the size of a tennis court with a bar. Black tables and leather-covered chairs surround the dance floor. Two bulky speakers fill the room with sounds of Spanish rumba tearjerkers; sometimes one of the guests grabs the mike and sings. The light show relies heavily on purple; four black-and-white landscapes evoking the bleakness of a Jim Jarmusch road movie hang on the walls to make up for the lack of windows. It smells of perfume, schnapps, and tobacco; the smoking room is right next door. We shake the hand of the bar owner, a broad-shouldered guy in a striped polo shirt and suit pants. His face looks incredibly like Al Bundy's, but a very serious Al Bundy without a trace of naivety—more mafia boss than comedian.

Vladimir confirms this impression with a fitting anecdote: "Don't mess with him. He was once beaten up on the street.

He drove home, changed his clothes because he didn't want to dirty his suit. He then went back to his assailant and shot him." I decide not to mess with him.

The next person I meet is a roughly seventy-year-old businessman with gold teeth, an arm in a cast, and the smell of alco-hol on his breath who quotes Heinrich Heine's "Die Lorelei":

I know not if there is a reason
Why I'm so sad at heart.[1]

While reciting he seems sincerely doleful. He then encourages me to knock back a number of cognacs and we head for the dance floor.

Other guests include a language professor from the university, an opera singer, and the head of a philosophy group.

Of course Vladimir knows them all. This underground pit is the meeting point of the town's high society. It somehow doesn't seem right to me, but then again, there are probably no alternatives.

★

MY *LANDSLEUTE*

RENAT, MY HOST in Makhachkala, is thirty-seven, an IT specialist, and has only had a driver's license for three months. He is looking forward to practicing his driving, so the next day we set off for a spin around the nearby villages in his Lada Granta. First we have to pass the October Revolution canal, which is pretty stinky because of a mountain of garbage on its banks. "We can fly to space, have the best ballet corps in the world, but we can't manage our own garbage disposal," Renat grumbles. "That's typically Russian; everyone moans about it and the next second they're chucking stuff away themselves."

Makhachkala is a monster of a city, a chaotic mix of stands selling shawarma and kvass (a beverage made of fermented rye bread), bridal gown stores, mosques, and colorful advertising posters. Only a few yards separate the drabness of Soviet tower blocks from the lively spectacle on the beaches of the Caspian Sea, with beach volleyball players, picnickers, swimmers, and brawny wrestlers all going about their business. The city has an official population of some 600,000, but according

to unofficial figures it could be twice that size; they seem to have somehow lost count.

We head south. At first the countryside gets greener and greener, then more mountainous. By the roadside there is a police post. "Shit, they'll stop us for sure," says Renat. "That'll ruin our whole day. They'll want all the paperwork, ask about our contacts and what we're doing here. They won't believe us whatever we say. Simple harassment." They don't stop us.

Renat has black-gray hair, brown eyes, and a dark complexion. He used to live in Langenfeld, Germany, in an asylum-seekers' hostel inside an ex-military compound. At that time many refugees were arriving from Dagestan because the region was affected by the Chechen wars. "I learned German from Jehovah's Witnesses; they were so patient in conversations. And from WDR 4"—a German radio station known for its sentimental playlist. "'Ich hab mein Herz in Heidelberg verloren' and other such songs; the sentences weren't too complicated." A pragmatic guy. He has very positive memories of Germany—jogging around the lake, the au pair girls from his language course, the rectitude of the officials. Also, he enjoyed the freedom of being far away from the clutches of family. "Parents in Dagestan try to control you until the day they die. They're afraid of letting go of their children, even when they are fifty or sixty."

Renat sometimes lapses into a highly original mixture of English and German: "My *Landsleute* explained me what to say and we *erfunden* bad situation," he says about making up a story for his talks with the asylum authorities. But when he went there, he got quite nervous: "I had the *schlechtes Gefühl* I do something *falsch*, and I think they *haben es gemerkt*." His grounds for asylum were rejected and he was deported. "I was

59

naive. If I had had internet at that time I would have gone about things more reasonably. Firstly I would have learned German and then applied for a place at university."

He has given up on the dream of a new start in Europe and now just hopes that the tension with Moscow doesn't intensify. "At the moment the situation in Ukraine is more critical, which is better for us; we are not the archenemy." Five or six years ago the situation was more acute; every crime committed with the involvement of someone from the Caucasus became a political issue. Or was made into one. "I was in Moscow in December 2010 as almost six thousand people demonstrated in Manezhnaya Square. Later it became violent. I was nearby and was shoved around by a group of men." The demo was in response to the murder of a Spartak Moscow soccer fan, who was shot during a brawl. The perp, a Caucasian, wasn't prosecuted and, according to rumors, had bribed the police.

The case launched a chain reaction that culminated in the demonstration on December 11, which attracted a diverse mix of nationalist groups and soccer hooligans. The mood became increasingly ugly, to the point where some participants began a random hunt for people who didn't look Slavonic. "Generally, it's not easy in Moscow if you look like me," Renat says dryly.

We drive on a dirt track between steep crags that rise from the grasslands like colossal fish fins. The road is lined by rainbow-sprinkled flowering meadows; the air smells of citrus fruits, the ground of cow dung. A huge eagle circles above us. Renat is highly demanding of his car, driving it through deep muddy pools and slaloming around rocks and small boulders. We drive with the constant expectation that we won't be able to carry on beyond the next serpentine twist because we don't have four-wheel drive. Shortly before the reception bars on my cell phone disappear, Vladimir calls to say that he pulled some strings and his contact is already waiting for us at the destination.

We reach Balkhar at midday. The village scores points for its spectacular setting on the mountainside and its quaint old men with hats sitting on a bench in the main square. Tiny, stooped babushkas return from the fields bearing wooden baskets full of tea leaves. Smelly cow pies are splattered on the stone walls of the houses to dry, later to be used as fuel. Donkeys, chickens, and cats roam around as a muezzin calls to prayer. I'm finding everything enchanting; Renat less so. "I don't understand why in this day and age people live in such remote places," he says. The locals belong to the Lak minority, who are well known for their handicraft skills, with a pottery tradition stretching back many centuries.

A B C
Domostroy · ДОМОСТРОЙ

A sixteenth-century Russian book on household rules, which in sixty-four chapters details instructions on how a moral citizen should behave. It's about godliness and obedience to the czar, but most of the rules are about living together as a family. For today's readers this collection is more of a curiosity than a practical guide, as much of the advice is outdated: "A man who loves his son will whip him often... Correct your son, and he will be a comfort in your old age and bring delight to your soul," or "A drunken man is an ill, but a drunken woman is utterly useless."[2]

61

A man of around sixty called Abakan, wearing a checked shirt and black vest, is there to greet us. "Vladimir has already told me of your arrival," he says, leading us to his workshop. On the floor there are enough brick-red pottery goats and horses to fill a medium-sized pharaoh's tomb; nearby, two women sit at wheels making small pots.

"We sell our wares at markets in towns. It's more lucrative than farming," explains Abakan.

Soon rain clouds loom and it begins to drizzle. We decide to make a move before the return route becomes impassable. When I have reception on my cell phone again I get an automatically relayed storm warning message: "Beware of storms and rain in the mountains of Dagestan, wind speeds of 18 meters per second to be expected."

Nevertheless, we stop one hour later in Shukty, another village in a sensational mountain landscape. The green areas beneath the craggy pinnacles seem so velvety and groomed, it's almost as if a groundskeeper were regularly caring for them. There are only two irritating things: First, there's an oil painting of Stalin at the memorial to the village's eighty-three World War II victims, possibly signifying a yearning for the good old days (for some reason, the dictator's forehead attracts many flies). Second, the whole slope is covered in three-story luxury houses—but 90 percent of them have neither doors nor windows, and it doesn't look as if anybody is planning to continue building.

A local entrepreneur and visionary, Magomed Chartayev, started a pilot project in Shukty. He was able to greatly increase productivity compared to other kolkhoz (collective farms) by sharing the profits from farming with the peasants; throughout the country, his village was heralded as an exemplary socialist project. Later he became wildly rich and donated two hundred houses to his village. Shukty came within a hair's breadth of being the most luxurious mountain village in Russia, but just before the houses were completed, Chartayev died. His sons were loath to invest further money from their inheritance in the village, and now most of the houses remain uninhabited.

Back in Makhachkala we pass a pub called Chende Choch, a Russian rendition of the German words for "hands up," which every Russian knows from war movies. The sign outside is, fittingly, an illustration of a machine gun. Clever people would deduce from this combination that visiting is not a good idea. I, on the other hand, insist on going there at all costs.

Renat's girlfriend, Katya, who has peroxide-blond hair, speaks perfect American English, and comes from Moscow, is all for it. A year previously she was his couchsurfing guest, and since then they have been a couple.

The pub is well patronized and smells of beer, smoke, and men's sweat, and smoked fish is hanging at the bar near the entrance. Soccer club pennants, photos of samba dancers at the Rio carnival, and a color printout of a Wikipedia article on FC Barcelona serve as decoration; hardly a square inch of the wall is free. The European Cup final soccer match between Portugal and France is playing on a small TV screen. Looking around I get the impression that almost all the guests are male, broad-shouldered, and five foot six, and that they have all agreed to sit at the table with the same laid-back posture, manspreading at an angle of roughly seventy degrees. They are probably discussing who shot whom, but that, of course, is pure speculation.

The waitress brings some pints of watery Port Petrovsk beer, and we ask for food. "We have so many orders that the fries need half an hour," she says. Behind her on the screen, Ronaldo is crying because a knee injury has forced him to be carried off the field. A short while later, a staggering guest is carted out of the pub by his friends in a similar manner; his problem is not his knee.

Food eventually arrives, forty-five minutes later. That time seems to have been spent continuously tossing the fries back and forth from salt to cheap cooking oil. Katya tries to make them a bit more palatable by digging for the deeper ones and wiping them individually on her napkin, but it doesn't help. The horseradish bread crackers are also extremely salty, and pieces of the *vobla* fish have a nasty habit of sticking to the teeth. I check on Wikipedia for what happens when you overdose on salt and am somewhat reassured.

Truth No. 4:
"A fatal dosage of table salt for adults is roughly equal to ten tablespoons. It is unlikely that this amount could be consumed accidentally."[3]

SO THIS EVENING ends with only two absences due to injuries. Portugal wins 1:0 but we decide unanimously not to make Chende Choch our favorite hangout.

RUSSIA

THE ELEVEN O'CLOCK bus to Elista is fully booked, says the dragon-like woman at *kassa* 1. Renat doesn't believe her; he walks directly to the bus and asks the driver. The driver says there is room and that it must have been a computer problem. The less dragon-like woman at *kassa* 2 sells me a ticket: 815 rubles, or US$14, for a twelve-hour ride. "Write down your name and place of birth." There you go.

The bus, from the Korean SsangYong group, visibly has more than two decades behind it. A fluorescent tube is attached vertically to the front windshield with adhesive tape; hopefully this is not a sign that the headlights aren't working. Seating numbers are written on yellow slips of paper and stuck on the rows with Scotch tape. A pennant with the Russian flag on one side and a bare-breasted model on the other hangs from the rearview mirror. I say my goodbyes to Renat and jump aboard.

A man of around fifty in a khaki shirt and Basque beret is sitting next to me by the window chewing sunflower seeds.

He has a wrinkled face, a fat belly, and a wart on his neck. "Germany good!" he says. "Dagestan: chaos and war." He slams his fists together. The bus sets off and before even reaching the main road the driver has lit up the first of many cigarettes, despite the No Smoking sign. The smoke somewhat overlays the smell of urine and sweat inside the bus. It begins raining outside and water soon begins to drip from the roof window. A passenger slams it shut, but the drips continue. The good news is that only one of the sixty seats is affected; the bad news is that it's mine.

Pretty soon my shoulder is completely wet. "Russia!" comments my neighbor, making a gesture as if throwing something away. Steady, large drops land on the headrest in front of me, exploding on contact into smaller drops and splashing me completely. It reminds me of an automatic sprinkler system, and watching it might be considered meditative if my shirt and pants weren't the final destination of the water. The steppe landscape outside doesn't offer much in terms of variety to distract me.

To my left my sunflower neighbor is spreading out; my right elbow is nestling on the sock of the sleeping man from the seat behind me, and because of the limited foot space there's no way of stretching out my knees. The only possible contortion consists of leaning my torso some twenty degrees forward, which would then enable my back to become sodden.

One lonely outpost in the middle of the steppes consisting of a few container-like buildings and a john marks the border between Dagestan and Kalmykia. "Desolate" would be a euphemism for this place. In the *kafe* the light goes out at the very instant I order my coffee. Power outage. In the darkness the waitress indicates that she can do nothing about it. "Russia," says the passenger next to me.

We continue for about fifty yards before the bus stops again. All passports have to be stacked at the front so an officer can check them. After a while, the bus driver suddenly shouts: "Shtefan! Nemezkiy!" That's me; nemezkiy means "German." I have to go to the police station. All the passengers' eyes follow me. I walk to the hexagonal building through pouring rain. Inside, an official with neatly trimmed light-brown hair is sitting behind a grille, which is so low that you have to duck submissively to look through it. In front of him is the screen of the surveillance camera; in the background a tube TV is running a shampoo commercial. The man has a couple of questions.

"What are you doing here?"

"I'm a tourist."

"And in Kalmykia?"

"Visiting a friend." A bit of an exaggeration as I don't yet know my next host. He demands her name and telephone number and writes both down on a list: Do svidanya, goodbye. I'm out of Dagestan.

The bus crosses the border to the only region in Europe where Buddhism is the majority religion. The driver starts a war movie. Dying soldiers on a tube TV; outside, Tibetan-looking stupas at dusk. The loudspeaker above me has a loose connection; the sound crackles loudly and from time to time cuts out altogether. Gun battle. Silence. Shouting soldiers. Crackle. Pause. "Russia," says my neighbor.

CHESS AND ALIENS

ALTANA LIVES WITH her mother in a new housing development called Microdistrict 9. The apartment is so clean and perfectly tidy that I hardly believe my eyes when I notice a small kink in the Tibetan prayer flag on the kitchen windowsill. In what seems to be an antiseptic living room from a furniture catalog, I somewhat hesitatingly deposit my slightly dirty backpack, trying to consider where I am least likely to disturb the feng shui. "You can take a shower, if you like," says Altana with polite urgency, opening the door to a bathroom composed of ceramics and brass that could well be used as the backdrop of an ad for faucet cleaner.

From dusty old Caucasus to germ-free *House Beautiful*, from Islam to Buddhism; the contrast with my previous destination couldn't be greater. And still I'm in Europe, a mere fifteen hundred miles from Berlin as the crow flies. Elista is closer to the German capital than the Canary Islands is.

Altana is twenty-three but looks at least five years younger; she has straight black hair, dark eyes, and Asian features. "I'm one hundred percent Russian. But when I travel everyone thinks I come from China or Japan," she says. Evenly spaced fridge magnets provide evidence of the countries she has visited: Spain, South Korea, England, France, Germany, and Turkey. From her online profile I know that she likes Tarantino movies, Kanye West, and The Beatles and that she has just completed her literature studies in Volgograd.

She only started "practicing couchsurfing" a few months previously. She says it as if she's talking about a religion. Her only guest before me came from Munich and was "extraordinarily friendly." But sometimes she gets strange inquiries. "A Spanish guy wrote me: 'How are you, wanna meet for tea?' When I checked his profile I discovered he was a porn movie producer who was looking for female performers. I concluded that I wouldn't meet him for tea."

Her mother, Yelena, joins us; she is a doctor and smiles a lot. "I speak little English," she says, smiling.

"You must be tired from the long bus journey," says Altana.

FROM A GLOBAL-HISTORY viewpoint the autonomous Republic of Kalmykia has, up to now, only played a minor role. Readers who have never heard of the autonomous Republic of Kalmykia are forgiven. Its inhabitants stem from Buddhist Oirat nomads from Mongolia who migrated toward the Volga in the seventeenth century. Initially they were tolerated, but one day Catherine the Great decided that she really was quite fond of her steppes. She ordered the building of forts and sent settlers, soldiers, and orthodox missionaries there.

The Oirats no longer felt welcome and planned, in the winter of 1771, to set out for western China, all at once and all on the same day. But only those living to the east of the Volga

69

actually made the long trek. Twenty thousand families to the west didn't dare cross the wide river because the ice didn't appear safe, and remained behind. *Kalmyk* means something like "the remainder."

For the next 150 years they were left in peace. Then the Bolsheviks swept through the country, wrecking Buddhist shrines and throwing monks into prisons. Religion, the opium of the people, was frowned on by Communists. When the Nazis arrived during World War II, roughly six thousand Kalmyks joined up as infantrymen. This in turn displeased Stalin so much that in 1943 he had almost the whole population of the republic deported to Siberia. Only fourteen years later did the survivors venture back. They have never been friends of Communism.

The autonomous Republic of Kalmykia, with Elista as its capital, has existed since 1992. For their recent development they have to thank a millionaire named Kirsan Ilyumzhinov, who was president of the republic until 2010 and would be a candidate for the title "most bizarre politician in modern times," even if the worldwide competition is strong. He became rich as director of a trading company in the chaotic '90s, and as a politician he was able to exploit the momentum of that time. The status of an autonomous republic enabled him to keep taxes low for businesses, much like an offshore trading platform. Thousands of companies registered in Kalmykia for an annual fee of US$23,500. Only in 2004 did the Duma decree that such loopholes would no longer be acceptable. Ilyumzhinov was able to get over it, as by that time he already owned four white Rolls-Royces.

Apart from all this he is well known for two things. First, in all seriousness he claims to have once been abducted in a flying saucer. Extraterrestrials dressed him in a yellow space suit, gave him a tour of their control center, and flew off to another star. He reported that he felt perfectly at ease with them, but eventually they had to transport him back so he would be on time for a political appointment in Ukraine. Second, Ilyumzhinov is one of his country's greatest chess fans and is still the president of the chess federation's governing body, FIDE.

In this capacity he was able to stage the 1998 Chess Olympiad in Elista. He was well connected to Boris Yeltsin, so with the equivalent of US$150 million from Moscow he built Chess City, a small villa district for competition players. In all the excitement and anticipation of the competition he completely forgot to plan what would be done with it after the tournament.

Chess City is only a few hundred meters away from Microdistrict 9. Altana doesn't feel like joining me; she thinks it is "a bit boring," although she, like all other Kalmyks, studied chess for three years as a compulsory subject at school. I set off alone in the ninety-five-degree heat, walking past a Tibetan temple and a large marquee-sized Mongolian yurt. The outer shell is made of air cushions and inside, according to the information board, will soon be a museum of the history of nomadic peoples. At the side of the road are sculptures made of light-colored stone blocks supposedly representing knights or pawns; probably, as they are roughly hewn and lack detail, they are meant to be incredibly avant-garde. To me, they seem to be simply unfinished.

In front of the visitor's parking at Chess City there is a kind of archway with the Russian name *Gorod Shakhmat*, which sounds like "checkmate." In a nutshell, the whole area seems

71

a bit checkmate. In the next hour I see a total of two cars and one pedestrian; otherwise the place is like a ghost town. I expected the houses might be numbered like a chessboard, with addresses like g6 and f4, that the streets might have names like Kasparov Crescent or Karpov Close, and that there would be pubs called The Queen's Head or The Castle Arms (in fact, the only pub here is called Flamingo, and it's closed today). But nothing of the sort—Checkmate City is a pretty nondescript new housing complex, although it's certainly not cheap to live here. The terraced houses have roofs in striking colors and small front gardens. There are a few faded posters of competitions with pictures of past chess heroes. Behind the walls, I imagine pipe-smoking men with long beards slamming down chess pieces on the board, full of passion. But most of the houses appear uninhabited and the only sound is the twittering of one single bird. This is a place of no past and no aura; here no one lived, loved, hated, was born, or died before it became shrouded in loneliness. Here a lot of money was simply poured down the drain.

Truth No. 5:
Nothing is more desolate than a ghost town without ghosts.

The Palace of Chess, in the center, with its semicircular foyer and reflective blue glass, looks a bit like a flying saucer. It was here that the competitions took place all those years ago. An armed security guard greets me at the entrance and soon I'm admiring the walls full of photo-realistic illustrations of people playing chess. Stylistically they are somewhere between local newspaper photos and children's book illustrations, and often ex-President Ilyumzhinov is in the picture.

On the third floor I find a kind of chess school, with wooden desks side by side in a classroom; on each of them there is a picture of a chessboard. The security guard calls me back, making a cross in front of him with his forearms to convey that visitors are not allowed there. Preferably they should go to the souvenir shop, where they can buy Buddhas and fridge magnets, slippers, plates with pictures of temples, and chess sets with Mongolian nomads serving as pawns and camels instead of knights.

"I see what you mean by 'boring,'" I say to Altana upon returning. Then we take a *marshrutka*, a routed taxicab minibus, downtown.

*

FREEDOM I

THE LARGEST BUDDHA in Europe lives in a shiny white temple with a square base and pointy gilt roofs, with Asian-style wooden pavilions surrounding it. "You should always circle the temple three times clockwise and spin the prayer wheels," explains Altana.

As we circle the temple there are quite a lot of prayer wheels—light-red cylinders with golden letters on them and small grips to make spinning them easier. All of them have been touched by the fourteenth Dalai Lama, who has been here a number of times. We take about five minutes to complete the 360-degree tour. "It's pretty hot today and it must be difficult for you, so I'd say one round is okay," decides Altana, who always knows what's good for me. We enter the inner room by passing through the entrance, which is marked by red columns beneath an eight-spoked Dharma wheel guarded by two wooden deer.

"What I like about Buddhism is that it's a free religion. Everyone can do or not do what they want and you are responsible for your own mistakes," says Altana. "In the temple, I find peace." At the end of the main hall to the left there is a framed picture of the Dalai Lama; in the middle sits a thirty-foot-high golden Buddha in a yellow cloak with crossed legs. He looks down from his lotus throne with a serious and contemplative expression. Aren't his facial features rather similar to those of the UFO enthusiast and shepherd of the Republic, Ilyumzhinov, who had the temple built for a vast sum of money? Pure coincidence, for sure. "You probably want to move on," says Altana.

I ask her what she thinks of Ilyumzhinov. "He wasn't as bad as people claim. His successor is doing absolutely nothing for progress."

"But with his alien stories he was a bit crazy, wasn't he?"

"Hey, that's Russia," says Altana, and laughs. "Anyway, politicians generally talk a lot of nonsense. Reports about aliens are by far not the worst!" Good point.

Truth No. 6:
The words "That's Russia" explain many things for which there is no logical explanation.

LATER WE MEET Vadim and Olga, two of Altana's friends. Vadim, on hearing that there was a German in town, definitely wanted to drink a beer with me. Immediately he tries out his language skills on me: "Heil Hitler. Sieg Heil. Hände Hoch. Das ist fantastisch." Only one of these four expressions upsets Olga. She laughs and asks him what kind of dirty movies he watches where they say things like "Das ist fantastisch"; he looks a bit sheepish. The restaurant-cum-multi-purpose-store sells not only fake DKNY and Dior handbags, but also a wide selection of beers in thirty-two-ounce cans and two-and-a-half-liter plastic bottles. A thirsty country. We go for the Zhigulevskoye beer; the label shows a busty lady carrying two very large beers on a silver tray, with gray prefabs and a Zhiguli car in the background.

Our surroundings are less dreary. There are housing blocks painted light red; a two-lane pedestrian path populated by twenty-year-old mothers with strollers and kids on hoverboards.

The spiral path to the "Exodus and Return" monument is laid out in such a way that you have to walk three times clockwise around the cuboid work of art before actually reaching it. The memorial shows marching groups of people with hardened, tired facial features, and things that are meant to relate to everyday life in Siberian exile, among them a giant fish, an embryo, and a bomb.

We sit on the pedestal and snap open the beers. "My grandma was in Siberia," Olga says. She is twenty-two, studied business administration, and now works as a bookkeeper. "It's unbelievable how hard life was there. She had to process timber, more than ten hours a day. But she survived and returned here."

The Elista before us consists of uniform housing complexes and an electric utility station. Behind them, plains stretch into the distance with isolated lights, and far, far off, a dark-red sun sinks to the horizon.

"Ten years ago all this was steppes, and we used to come here as kids for picnics," says Altana. The place has changed; it's becoming more modern, but still the younger generation dream of escaping, unlike their parents' and grandparents' generations, with their memories of hardship in exile. Olga says that she would love to live in Provence. "I love dancing," she says, "but in Elista there are only strange clubs where you have to watch out for drunks. I was in South Korea once, there it was totally different—every night we were out and about."

Seoul instead of Siberia—the younger people are happy they were born after the collapse of the Soviet Union. "The freedom is good; we don't want to go back. But there are still many constraints. Hardly anyone has a job that they really enjoy," says Olga. "And Elista really is pretty boring." We sit for a while in silence, drinking and looking into the twilight until the sun disappears behind the electric utility. "You must be tired," says Altana at last.

FREEDOM II

A **"FREE TRAVELER" IS,** according to Anton Krotov's definition, someone who spends not more than half of his traveling time with people who are paid to cater to the traveler's needs. He includes not only tourist guides and hotel receptionists, but also bus drivers and baristas in cafés.

Krotov is famous among Russian backpackers, a guru who founded the "Academy of Free Travelers" and has sold 150,000 copies of his hitchhikers' guide for adventurers. I met him eight years ago on a short visit to Moscow and slept for two nights on his living-room floor.

The term "free" has two meanings for him: first, making do with as little money as possible, and second, staying away from tourist attractions. "Most Europeans just hang around the whole time in cafés and think they're traveling," is one of his sentences that I've remembered to this day. Another is: "A quick tongue will get you everywhere." He is living proof of that one, and has even managed to blag his way to free rides on ships, long-distance trains, and freight planes.

Krotov's most important finding after traveling almost 400,000 miles: the world isn't such an inhospitable place, as claimed by "frightened journalists who take foolhardy risks and then report on how dangerous everything is."

After he had experienced, hundreds of times, how hospitably people received total strangers, Krotov came up with the concept of "House for Everyone." He rents cheap properties for two or three months in Cairo, Dushanbe, Berlin, or Irkutsk and opens them up to people who want to spend the night there for free. There are, however, conditions: clear rules and an authoritarian leadership structure is intended to ensure that living together proceeds in a civilized manner, that everyone shares the chores, and that no drugs or alcohol are consumed. It's a socialist experiment for travelers that is in part financed by donations from the guests.

At the moment House for Everyone is located in the Babayevsky District in northeastern Astrakhan, which I reach after a four-and-a-half-hour bus trip from Elista. Krotov himself isn't managing this project, but one of his supporters, twenty-four-year-old Alexei, is. He sent me instructions on how to get there from downtown, seventeen rubles by bus. I'm pretty tired and briefly consider taking a taxi (five hundred rubles for a twenty-minute trip, roughly the equivalent of eight U.S. dollars), but that wouldn't feel right on the way to visit such dedicated travelers.

Thanks to an app called Maps.me, developed by a Russian programmer, journeys on public transport to a foreign destination are not as exciting as they were ten years ago. Then, you had to continually pester fellow passengers with questions—are we already there, how far is it—while trying to decipher signposts outside. Nowadays I just look at my cell phone.

I download the map to my next destination from Maps.me when I have a wireless connection. Then a reliable blue arrow shows where I am at that moment. This works as long as my cell phone reception does, and even sometimes, as if by magic, in dead spots. Getting really lost was much easier in the old days.

"Nowadays I just look at my cell phone," I admit, is not a pretty sentence. Where is the interaction with the locals, the alert looking through windows, the total immersion in a country without digital distractions? How on earth did a smartphone with a local SIM card become an indispensable part of one's luggage when traveling? One hundred and thirteen grams of stainless steel, microchips, and plastic have replaced telephone kiosks, travel agencies, encyclopedias, maps, dictionaries, camcorders, compasses, notepads, newspapers, and internet cafés. Believe me, Marco Polo or Roald Amundsen would have packed an iPhone or a Samsung Galaxy had they been available. Both of them traveled with the most modern equipment of their times.

Still, sometimes I do mourn the good old days of "real" adventure; but then I wipe the teardrops off the touchscreen, scroll through my contacts, and remember all those fantastic memories from spending time with people I would never have met without the internet. In purely mathematical terms it's worth the effort. I spend more hours with people I have found online than I lose looking for them, even though on average I have to send out three couch requests for every positive answer. But as soon as I enter the apartment of the next host, I turn my cell phone off.

ASTRAKHAN IS ON the Volga and looks like most other Russian cities: castle-like train station, a couple of onion-like domes, a large "Great Patriotic War" memorial park and lots of prefab buildings. I can't help thinking of the 1975 movie *The Irony of Fate*, which is always shown on New Year's Day in Russia. It's about a group of friends meeting in a *banya*, a public sauna, to celebrate New Year's Eve; they get very drunk and mistakenly put the wrong person on a plane. The next morning, the main character wakes up in Leningrad instead of Moscow and doesn't notice the slightest difference. The housing blocks, the street names, the apartments, even the furniture, are all exactly the same as in his home city; even the front door key fits.

Unlike the guy in the movie, I'm thankfully in the right city; the instructions have brought me to my destination. After a twenty-minute bus trip, a ten-minute walk, eight floors up in an elevator, and one floor using the stairway (for some inexplicable reason the elevator doesn't go all the way to the top), Alexei opens the door. "Ninety-two square meters, 12,000 rubles a month," he says proudly, showing me around. There is a living room, a communal kitchen, a room for Alexei and his wife, three rooms with beds, and the possibility of sleeping on the floor. Beige and shades of brown dominate; the floorboards creak musically; the electric cables on the walls and ceilings look horrifyingly improvised. If we were in Berlin a realtor would describe it as "a charming historic building ideal for fans of 'ostalgia'"—the German concept of nostalgia for aspects of life in East Germany—and be overwhelmed with offers. There are travel photos on the walls featuring Alexei, or Anton Krotov, or both of them together, in distant countries: Afghanistan, Pakistan, Bangladesh, India, China.

Alexei, a burly guy with short hair and a goatee, is wearing a T-shirt depicting the flags of the ten member countries of the Association of Southeast Asian Nations (ASEAN). "I've been to all of them except Brunei," he declares proudly. All in all he has visited thirty-nine countries and seventy-nine of Russia's eighty-five regions. He likes talking about where it is easiest to apply for a visa. Laos and Vietnam are no problem at all for Russian travelers, as they were former allies of the Communists. Germany, on the other hand, is particularly difficult, and Australia is a tough nut as well. Alexei is about to start a small lecture tour with travel tips, has written a book about Burma, and sometimes works as a tour guide on Phuket in Thailand.

Gradually I get to know my fellow lodgers, who greet me en passant. At the moment there are three Russian travelers here along with Alexei and his wife, Alena, who married shortly after her eighteenth birthday and have always traveled together since then. He tells me that Morocco, Senegal, and Gabon are their next destinations. But first of all he is caretaking the House for Everyone for another two months.

On our first tour of the premises I notice many signs tacked to the walls with the house rules.

No noise, please!

Don't leave the floor wet!

Save water!

How to wash dishes: Just wash everything you see, thanks!

Don't speak in the hallway! Walk lightly!

Don't smoke! Churchill was a smoker—dead. Lenin never smoked—he lives on.

Use the stairs! The elevator often breaks down and disturbs the peace.

Don't wash feet in the sinks!

Don't leave hair in the sinks! There are no servants here!

Maximum of five minutes in the john, maximum of ten minutes in the shower!

No stamping of feet!

After 10:00 PM talk quietly, after 11:00 PM complete quiet!

When at 10:30 I drop my SLR and it lands to the floor with a crash, I feel like a troublemaker; at 11:37 as I sneak into the bathroom to brush my teeth, I feel like a criminal.

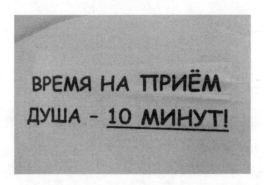

Truth No. 7:
In practice, socialism means more constraints than the theory suggests.

Was I enthusing earlier about smartphones replacing travel agencies? A Russian-language beginner looking for a real challenge should try booking a train ticket on a Russian website on a cell phone. With the aid of Google Translate it's perfectly feasible, but very time-consuming.

In the process I learn the following vocabulary: Отчество (middle name). Иностранный Документ (foreign passport). Дата рождения (date of birth). Места для пассажиров с животными (seats for passengers with pets). Купить билеты (buy tickets). Резервирование билетов (reserve tickets). Ошибка (error). платеж не прошел (payment failed). Shit. Back to the beginning. On the second attempt, again my credit card is not accepted. The promise of saving time by not having to line up at a ticket office had proved too good to be true. I take a bus to the station,

83

and after waiting some forty minutes I finally have my *plazkart* ticket for the night train to Volgograd in my hands, carriage 2, bed 16.

A B C
Eclipse

The name of a 533-foot-long luxury motor yacht built by Blohm & Voss in Hamburg. It belongs to the Russian oligarch Roman Abramovich. His instructions while it was in the process of being constructed offered interesting insights into the psyche of the multimillionaire who has everything. Twice he ordered the lengthening of his boat to regain the record from the *M/Y Dubai*, which was being built by the same shipbuilders for Sheikh Mohammed bin Rashid Al Maktoum, the ruler of Dubai. In 2009 Abramovich eventually won the Longest Luxury Yacht competition between sheikh and oligarch by twenty inches. Four years later he was trumped by another sheikh ship, the 590-foot-long *Azzam*.

Plazkart is the cheapest ticket category—an open-plan carriage with bunk beds. People willing to pay more sleep in a *kupe*, a compartment with a sliding door for two to four people.

I board the ten o'clock train at ten-thirty, which is possible as all long-distance trains in the country run on Moscow time and Astrakhan is one hour ahead. Every coach is guarded by a uniformed *provodniza*, the conductress and undoubted sole authority over the carriage, who checks tickets and passports.

Once you're past her, the real tests are still to come—stowing luggage beneath the lowest bunk in a small closet, changing out of hiking boots and into flip-flops (beginners will find them, of course, at the bottom of their backpacks), rolling out the mattress and putting on the sheets, and finally, finding a position that is reasonably comfortable. I have particular problems with the latter as at six foot two I seem to exceed the average size of Russian travelers. On the top bunk I'm unable to sit upright and if I stretch out, both my feet hang in the aisle at exactly the head height of passing passengers. A well-intended metal security bar along the edge of the bed prevents a lethal fall, but also means that when I lie on my side, there's not enough room for my knees. I practice experimental night-train yoga for nine long hours in an attempt to find the best position to stow my torso and limbs in an orthopedically optimal manner. Result: lying on my back, one knee slightly bent and to the left, resting on the wall. In this position I reach Volgograd.

ONE PERCENT

AS SOON AS you exit the station there's no doubt about what, from a historical viewpoint, is important here. Souvenir stalls sell mugs with war motifs, victory statuettes, and Stalin figures; a huge information board depicts a map with the cities and towns involved in the Battle of Stalingrad, the name of Volgograd until 1961. The entrance to the station is flanked by two tableaux of soldiers with arms at the ready. They are positioned in such a way as to suggest that danger is coming from one of the lampposts nearby.

My hosts are named Sergei, Krisia, and Grisha, and are fifty-five, thirty-seven, and three years old, respectively. In his profile Sergei included a quotation from his mother, which I liked: "A maximum of one percent of people are absolutely wonderful and perfect and one percent are totally evil. The remaining ninety-eight percent are a complicated mixture of good and bad. In life you usually meet people who are neither angels nor devils but a mixture of both. If you want to live among angels you have to prompt them to show only their good sides."

In my travels I have experienced this to be true. In particular, in countries on the receiving end of negative press, I have often experienced the most wonderful things with ordinary people, which don't appear to match the bad image projected in the media. I find these statistics totally plausible, even at the bottom end. It's perfectly possible that one percent of Russians are complete and utter dorks. And one percent of Austrians, one percent of Muslims, one percent of Americans, one percent of Germans, one percent of Christians, one percent of Nigerians, one percent of refugees, one percent of women, one percent of left-handers. Unfortunately this one percent often generates a great deal of attention. And even though the proportion is very small, mathematically, with a global population of 7.4 billion, we arrive at 74 million idiots worldwide. That's enough to cause quite a bit of damage.

Sergei is actually a historian, but works as a cab driver. He has a mustache and many laugh lines and radiates down-to-earth warmth. If Russia were a fairground, he would be the much-beloved organ-grinder away from the hurly-burly. At home he likes to display his extensive belly by only wearing swimming shorts. Krisia also has a large belly, but for different reasons. "It wasn't planned; I already have two kids, Sergei and Grisha," she quips. "Oh, can you take care of the boy for fifteen minutes? We have to drop in on the neighbors briefly."

Of course I can. But as soon as the door closes the absence of his mother seems to trigger a certain unease in Grisha. First he tests how often you have to *brrrm* a toy car along the floor before it loses its wheels (result: thirteen times). He then begins to select single CDs from their plastic case to test their suitability as Frisbees in various rooms. I try a diversionary tactic with a foam ball that was lying around, and he is immediately distracted from the shiny discs. He pops the ball in his mouth and with obviously suicidal intent crawls into a large plastic bag. After I prohibit this, the little lemming dashes to the kitchen and climbs on the sill of an open window. There, he tries to shake the wooden safety grille loose; outside it's four floors to the ground.

Truth No. 8:
Fifteen minutes can be an eternity.

"Was Grisha well-behaved?" asks Krisia on her return.

"Yes, a remarkable boy," I reply.

The plan for the rest of the day is made quickly: buy fish and beer, then watch a movie. In a small store we get a number of one-and-a-half-liter plastic bottles filled with "Bavaria" beer and buy warm smoked milkfish and cold smoked bream. Russian liquor stores often have a fish display and smell accordingly. At home we spread it all out on newspaper.

A B C

Frau Schmidt

The name of a powder detergent that's produced in Russia, though consumers are led to believe it's a quality product "Made in Germany." One of its competitors is called *Meine Liebe* (My Love); it's described in German on the package as "a gel for washing black and dark materials." The slogan accompanying *Gruntaler* cheese is slightly more cryptic and promises, in good old Google Translate fashion: "Tastes of spice herbs—delicate spiciness, tart flowering." In a well-stocked Russian shopping center you can find suits from *Kanzler* (Chancellor), butter from *Danke Anke* (Thanks, Anke), muesli from *Dr. Körner* (Doctor Grains), stationery from *Erich Krause*, *Bork* electronic goods, and *Altstein* beer. All these products are made somewhere, but not in Germany. Find this dishonest? Then look and see how many fictitious Russian-sounding names you can find on the vodka shelf of your local supermarket.

Another guest rings the doorbell, a full-bearded New Zealander named David on a world tour. He pulls up a seat in the kitchen, marveling at the notes of thanks and mottos that Sergei's previous guests have scribbled on the wall in felt tip. Why does he enjoy having guests so much? "I'm a hunter, a fisherman, and you are my victims. You've become caught in my net and I'm going to drink your blood." Then he toasts us. "To fishing!" The victims from New Zealand and Germany look slightly puzzled at the man in his underwear. "What I mean," says Sergei, "is the certainty that you are more interesting than my neighbor. If you were normal you wouldn't be traveling here. Cheers!" That sounds a little bit better.

A few minutes later, as Sergei boots up his laptop and starts a movie on YouTube, it really is the end of normality. "This is my favorite movie, Nebyvalshchina, from 1983, I've watched it twenty-three times. Once you've seen it, you know everything there is to know about mankind."

Well then, it's time to give it a good watch. The English title of the movie is Believe It or Not and the action takes place on a small farmstead: pigtailed women with long skirts, wooden huts, wheat fields, nineteenth century. The main characters are an idiot, a soldier, and an inventor. To begin with all the men on the farmstead are away at war. Except for the idiot, who looks a bit like a young Boris Johnson, who seizes the opportunity of lack of competition to get married. What follows is one of the saddest love scenes in the history of movies. A straw floor, both wearing long-sleeved pajamas; they gaze into emptiness, an embarrassed silence, a little peck on the cheek, he yawns, she smiles. Cut.

Enter the inventor. He looks like a barefooted Klaus Kinski in rags. With feverish fervor he empties the feathers from a cushion to attach them to a pair of wooden artificial wings. He attaches them to his arms and amid the jeering of the village youth, he Icaruses into the water from a ledge. Later he experiments with a hot-air balloon in the shape of a cow and a rocket made out of pickled gherkin fibers, powered by gunpowder. Both experiments go disastrously wrong.

The plot really starts to go haywire upon the appearance of the soldier, who looks like Chris Evans. A strange king with a high-pitched voice and a speech defect appears and puts on a gas mask because of the soldiers' smelly socks whereupon all his courtiers, also wearing gas masks, begin fiercely fighting. A hole to Hell opens up in the floor and Boris, Klaus, and Chris tumble into it and find themselves in a wild orgy with a bunch of hot witches in a kind of *banya* steam room before the Devil drives them out. There then follows a failed attempt to reach Heaven via a dangling rope, a masked ball in the snow, and more fighting.

In the final scene the inventor, using supernatural powers, eventually manages to fly and the soldier invites people to his magic show. To the left, old men and women creep under the magic table and, after a blow of a hammer on an anvil, reappear to the right, skipping out as young children. It is, of course, just a trick, as the elderly people are later unveiled hidden beneath the tablecloth. The last to pass through is the idiot: on the other side, a naked child skips out, and under the table: nothing. The idiot is transformed; in his new body he runs off toward the horizon. The End.

A farming community populated by ambitious idiots wreaking nothing but chaos between Heaven and Hell and solving conflicts with beatings. Interesting view of mankind. But maybe in a place like Volgograd it's not so easy to have a high opinion of one's own species.

★

NOVEMBER 1942

THE WAY TO the angriest mother in the world is up two hundred steps, one for every day of the Battle of Stalingrad, and past the Hall of Military Glory, which is always guarded by two sentries on wooden podiums. For the ceremony of changing of the guards they march in a goose-step. Before a guard is relieved, sweat is wiped from his face by an officer, who then tucks the cloth he used into the guard's side pocket. The circular hall displays the names of fallen soldiers and their ranks on mosaic stones hammered into the wall. In the middle of the hall there is a huge hand made of white concrete holding a torch, which has been burning continuously since before the sentries were born.

Outside, the rat-a-tat of machine-gun fire comes from invisible speakers. The path leads past neatly trimmed lawns and heroes' gravestones to the highest point on Mamayev Kurgan, the hill where the imposing statue *The Motherland Calls* stands: a tower-high avenging spirit with robes streaming out behind her, face contorted with anger, and mouth wide open.

What a clamor it would make if a being this size really were to scream! The right arm waves a sword in the air, as long as the fuselage of a Boeing 737; the left arm is stretched out horizontally with an open hand—an order to her own troops to fight, or maybe also a reproachful gesture toward her enemies. The statue represents Russia in the fall of 1942 as German troops were advancing toward Stalingrad, and symbolizes the Red Army's most important military triumph in the Great Patriotic War.

Including her sword, the concrete lady is 279 feet high. The Statue of Liberty in New York (151 feet) or Christ the Redeemer in Rio (98 feet) would seem like small children next to her; symbolically, of course, such a triumvirate would be nonsensical, as neither liberty nor Jesus enjoyed much favor with Stalin. "That's pretty much the most impressive statue I've ever seen," says David, who is exploring the city with me. Mamayev Kurgan, simply called "Height 102" on maps of the time, was the scene of some of the toughest fighting in the city and was covered in trenches, minefields, and barbed wire. The blood of more than thirty thousand dead soldiers seeped into the ground here.

We travel to the Stalingrad Museum in a quaint subway that looks like an old-fashioned streetcar. The museum is located directly adjacent to remnants of the brick walls of Grudinin's Mill—the only building that was left untouched after the war, which has been preserved as a memorial, rather like the A-Bomb Dome in Hiroshima. In front of it, six children sculpted from light-colored stone are dancing on a fountain around a crocodile. I recognize them from one of the most famous photos of Stalingrad: it shows this sculpture, which had somehow miraculously survived the house-to-house fighting and destruction all around. Thanks to the replica erected here, everyone can snap a similar photo—children circling and jeering at a predator against a backdrop of ruins. All that is missing is the fire in the windows, the smoke, and the dust.

David is more interested in the tanks and artillery a few yards away. "Can you take a picture of me?" Yes, I can. David on an 88-mm flak gun, David on a T-34 tank, David on a 150-mm heavy howitzer 18. He finds it "awesome" and wonders why I'm not interested in posing for similar photos—especially as a German.

I don't need them. In the attic of my grandpa's house there are enough memories of Stalingrad, tidily stowed in a small tin box: one crumpled map of the city, scale 1:100,000; a soldier's German–Russian dictionary; a translation of one of Stalin's radio broadcasts; one Iron Cross, second class; one Iron Cross, first class; a General Assault Badge in silver; a wounded badge and notification that on November 9, 1942, he was transported from Stalingrad to a military hospital in Luxembourg suffering from infectious yellow fever (*Hepatitis epidemica*). He never explained how he got his medals. Up until his death in 1981 he never spoke of the war—maybe out of shame, maybe self-protection, maybe because he didn't want to burden his offspring.

November 9, 1942. At that time everything was pointing to an imminent victory by the Germans, even though they were less well-equipped for the oncoming winter than their enemies. The Germans had already conquered large parts of the city, as shown by an expensive 3-D animation in one of the museum's exhibition rooms. But fortunes turned ten days later with Operation Uranus: the Germans were surrounded; the Russians gained the upper hand and held on to their advantage until Field Marshal Friedrich Paulus capitulated in January 1943. It's quite possible that yellow fever saved my grandpa's life.

The museum displays weapons, uniforms, newspaper cuttings, bravery medals, and endless rows of black-and-white portraits of war heroes. A monotone voice from the audio guide explains the exhibits and relics. Particularly interesting is a "lithographic stone, which was prepared in advance by Hitler's soldiers," as the voice informs me. This was the printing plate for pamphlets only in Russian. The title on it reads: "STALINGRAD HAS FALLEN." Proof of the degree of optimism of the German army, which was used to victory, upon arriving on the Volga. Hitler expected Stalingrad to fall within eight days; nobody in Germany thought that it might take months or that overwintering would be necessary.

The printing plate identifies Moscow as the "head" of the Soviet Union and Stalingrad as its "heart." The accompanying illustration shows a huge knife marking the location of the city on a map. Beneath a swastika banner, a victory that never took place is described: "The Russian government recently boasted that this city with 448,000 inhabitants and with the most important communication facilities in the country would never fall into German hands. Now the supply lines along the Volga, Europe's longest river, have been stopped."

But, as we know, history took a different turn. The printing plate was never used. In the end Stalingrad cost the lives of 500,000 Russians and 150,000 Germans. "That's the most awesome museum I've ever seen," says David at the exit, with a gleam in his eye.

In the evening it's fish and beer again with Sergei and Krisia; later, vodka and cognac due to a surprise visit by two of their friends from Chelyabinsk.

For certain nationalities, you can pinpoint activities or situations where they seem to be totally at ease and in their natural element. In tune with their world, free from all insecurity, distraction, or routine lethargy. Cubans are like this when they dance, or the Chinese when they're at a fully laden table. For Russians, it's when they have schnapps glasses in their hands and are about to propose a toast. At least on this evening, it is unmistakable.

Sergei teaches me a few Russian songs on the guitar; we sing and drink and eat and sing and drink.

"These are pretty much the nicest people I've ever met," says David.

★

A CAB ODYSSEY

I TAKE A DIRECT flight from the former conflict zone of Volgograd to today's conflict zone: the Crimean Peninsula. It's a hard landing, but the passengers still clap. My cell phone immediately finds a Russian network; it's called WIN, which sounds portentous. I deliberated a long time about whether to include this stop on my itinerary, because my entry from Russia is considered an illegal border crossing by the Ukrainians. And aren't all tourists using this route implying that they recognize the new rulers from Moscow, that they in some way condone the annexation? I don't like either option, but in the end my curiosity wins.

If there is such a thing as travel karma, then shortly after leaving Simferopol International Airport I am punished. Late in the evening, heading across a dark parking lot to a bus stop, I am addressed by a man. He has a female passenger in his cab already, he says. He offers me a ride, saying that I could share the price of the trip with her. I tell him the address and he nods.

The cab driver is middle-aged, has brown skin, and wears a hoodie, pants, and sneakers in various hues of gray. His cab, a gas-powered Chinese Geely CK, seems okay, but there is no cab sign. I get in the back; the front seat is occupied by the woman, who looks around thirty. Mistake number one: taking an unmarked taxi in which—mistake number two: there are other passengers. There are occasional warnings about this in guidebooks on Russia. Mistake number three: Alex—the name of the young man who gets in next to me. Didn't the driver say there was only *one* passenger traveling with us?

Alex is an athletic-looking young guy in a pink T-shirt and Adidas shoes who smells of cigarettes and beer and, immediately after greeting me, launches into a detailed monologue about the breasts and butts of Crimean women. The visual support for his third-class-English locker-room drivel is provided by his lewd groping of the air. *Thank God I don't have far to go*, I think.

After fifteen minutes, however, the map on my smartphone tells me that we're a couple miles beyond my destination. I assume the woman is being dropped off at home first. But as we take the overland road out of the city and the driver puts his foot on the gas, I begin to feel uneasy. I tell him my destination again. "Simferopol? Not Sevastopol?" asks Alex. "Are you sure?" I am. Was there a misunderstanding? The driver makes no effort to turn around; in fact, he even accelerates a bit. Anger improves language skills and I shout to the man in the front: *"Ya skazal Simferopol, nyet Sevastopol!"*

But my Russian is not good enough to understand his answer. Unfortunately Alex the air-groping breast fiend is the only one who speaks a bit of English, so I will have to make use of him as an interpreter. The driver explains that he is now too far outside Simferopol, so he doesn't want to turn back now. However, as he lives in Simferopol, he will drive to the next destination and drop me off later. "How long will it take?" I demand. "A hundred miles there and back, two hours," Alex translates the answer. It's already nearly midnight.

I feel even more uneasy. Are Alex and the driver in on something together? Do they plan to mug me and leave me in the gutter? What exactly was the reason for the German Foreign Office advising against visits to Crimea? My cell phone battery is already very low, so I don't read up on the reasons; maybe I'll need the map app later.

We stop to refuel at a gas station belonging to the local company in Bakhchysarai, TES; their logo is a white elephant against a purple background who is grinning like he's high from sniffing too much gasoline. When traveling, I sometimes imagine that shortly before I arrive somewhere a small armada of stage designers have prepared the scene for my arrival. This time, I would have to take them to task: the image of the elephant really does *not* match the seriousness of the situation.

We get out and I call my host in Simferopol to explain the situation and ask him whether I should leave and take a cab back from here. He says that at this time of night it's tricky finding cabs. I pass my cell phone to the driver so he can relay his planned route. After that, my host says he doesn't think the man sounds like a crook. So I get back into the car. The driver, totally placid, washes all the windows; Alex smokes. I seem to be the only one interested in reaching my destination in the near future.

At 12:22 AM I spot the first Putin poster at the side of the road; at 12:30 AM, the first machine gun. It's in the hands of a man with a face mask standing next to a police car and its occupants.

"How are you feeling?" asks Alex, his hand brushing my shoulder while he looks at me probingly. "Not so good?" His sudden empathy seems horrifyingly implausible. In terms of acting, the way he rearranges his facial muscles from empathy to compassionate indignation is even less successful. "*Such a silly situation, yes!*" For a moment the image of the roadside ditch looms again. His following attempts at small talk (trying to calm down the victim?) don't improve things.

"Where do you come from?"

"Hamburg."

"Nice. Lots of water. Like Saint Petersburg."

Five minutes later: "Do you like the music?" He nods towards the car radio, which is playing an anthem from the Italo-slush bard Eros Ramazzotti.

Me: "So-so."

Him: "I like this song."

Silence.

I notice that his T-shirt is very tight and his shaved face unusually well taken care of. "Maybe you'd like to spend the night in my dacha and take the bus tomorrow? One hundred forty rubles."

"No, thanks."

Silence. Secretly I wish he'd start talking about tits again.

Ahead of us the lights of a city become visible. Sevastopol. A triumphal arch with the inscription 1783–1983 commemorates the two hundredth anniversary of the penultimate Russian annexation of Crimea. At that time Catherine the Great tricked the Ottoman Empire out of the region. In front of the entrance to the Grand Hotel Ukraina there are billboards advertising a table-dance bar. We pass sinister-looking memorials for some war heroes or another, and a striking number of trees by the roadside; we can smell the sea. Until 1991 the city was barred to foreigners as the Black Sea fleet was stationed here. The driver puts his foot down as the front-seat passenger gives directions to the place she wants to be dropped. He stops, she pays, and they say their goodbyes.

There's no longer an obtrusive witness. We cross the whole city, reaching a kind of industrial zone. The street is no longer asphalted, and the last lamppost is far behind us; to the right is a huge parking area full of military trucks.

Some five minutes later we reach a barrier. A guard lifts it and once again we are in a residential area. Expensive houses with high walls and suvs parked outside, but the street remains an uneven dirt track. Alex directs the driver through a labyrinth of small alleys.

We stop; Alex wishes me a nice trip and bows out with a handshake that lasts slightly longer than necessary.

I exhale in relief. Not kidnapped, then. "Come and sit in the front, my friend," says the driver. "My name is Yuri. Poyekhali— let's go!" He looks at me critically to see whether I understood the reference. His namesake, Yuri Gagarin, the first man in space, said this single word just before takeoff.

"Poyekhali," I agree tiredly. He then drives me to my destination at rocket speed.

★
WARSHIPS

AFTER A SHORT night in Simferopol with a host who was surprisingly understanding about my late arrival, I travel by bus the next day past the elephant gas station again. My next destination is a village near Bakhchysarai, where Alisa, her husband, Konstantin, and their three children await me in a cozy wooden house that looks like somewhere Pippi Longstocking would have lived.

I stow my luggage. "Do you want to do a tour around Sevastopol?" asks Alisa. Her neighbor is going there for shopping in her pickup and has some spare seats. "Sounds great," I reply. Alisa has dark, serious eyes, long black hair, and the quiet, refined manners of an introverted artist who would rather let her work do the speaking than stand in the foreground. She wrote a children's book about Crimea and illustrated it with watercolors. Some of her illustrations are being shown in an exhibition at the moment. She also works as a translator to earn money.

We drive past impressive table mountains with vertical cliff faces, on which proficient rock climbers could have a lot of fun.

The rocks gleam almost white in the harsh midday sun and trees cling to the not-too-steep areas.

The news messages on my cell phone are less appealing than the landscape: "Russia's security agency, the FSB, thwarted a terrorist attack in Crimea planned by Ukrainian agents," writes RT. "The objective of the foiled attack in Crimea—'the death of tourism,'" writes *Sputnik*. "Crimean crisis: worries about a new war," writes *Spiegel Online*. Well, I've really chosen a good time to visit. A group of Ukrainians carrying ninety pounds of explosives are said to have tried to reach Crimea. According to the Russians they were stopped at the border, and two border guards were killed in the exchange of fire. The information couldn't be verified independently. What is certain is that this incident will intensify the crisis between Ukraine and Russia. I ask Alisa if she is worried and she answers: "I don't follow the news, it's just too depressing."

There are enough other things to read, anyway. For example, the quotes on the Putin posters on the side of the main road: "The opening of the highway and train bridge between Crimea and the Caucasus is planned for December 18, 2018. We have to fulfill this historic mission." "... the program for the development of Sevastopol's military base and the Black Sea fleet will be implemented," "Our aim is to make Crimea and Sevastopol the most modern and dynamic development regions in Russia." A lot of time will pass, particularly in the case of the latter promise, until all this is realized; you can see that on every street corner. But Sevastopol, despite its dilapidated buildings, has not lost its atmosphere of a fashionable coastal city. The "White City" on the Black Sea sparkles even though its plaster is crumbling. Should the situation ease, the property developers will come flocking back.

We get out at the covered market in the city center. Oranges and apples, lettuce, dried fruits, and nuts are all presented in opulent displays. And Yalta onions, slightly sweet, red, and shaped like a flattened mini squash. Even more interesting are the T-shirt stores at the entrance. "Not as many Putin designs as I thought," says Alisa. But the president does appear a few times, once holding a puppy in his arms and once with 007 sunglasses.

More unusual is the shirt printed with "Politeness can conquer a city" next to a screened photo of a soldier in a green helmet and goggles, his arms cradling a terrifying weapon. On his back he appears at first to have angel wings, but on closer inspection they turn out to be the spread-eagle wings of the Russian crest.

At the beginning of 2014 such soldiers (okay, minus the wings) suddenly appeared everywhere in Crimea, without emblems on their uniforms. Soon they were being referred to as the "polite people" because these seemingly military-looking men stressed unaggressive behavior; they didn't steal fruit from strangers' gardens and were perfectly willing to pose for souvenir photos.

On the basis of their other nickname you could say that Crimea, for the first time in human history, was the scene of an invasion of "little green men," but that would be badly downplaying the situation at the time. Their origins were eventually clarified. President Putin admitted at an annual televised press conference that in some instances there was some sort of involvement of soldiers coming from Russia.

At that time Alisa hardly noticed the "little green men" as her village is so remote that they never appeared there. "But suddenly a couple of strangers who none of us had ever seen came to inspect the village. I think they were just saying: we are now your new friends and we're here to protect you."

What has changed since the annexation by Russia?

"Life has become more expensive. And many popular products from Ukraine are no longer available. Sunflower oil, dairy products, vegetables." Also, eBay and Amazon don't work anymore. And to cross the mainland border—Alisa originally comes from Minsk in Belarus—she needs a verifiable reason, such as the funeral of a relative. Otherwise the only option is a circuitous flight via Moscow; even then there are snags when booking. Credit cards are often rejected when an online portal has an IP address from Crimea. I have similar problems when trying to arrange my flight to Saint Petersburg; I'm unable to pay and have to ask a friend in Hamburg to make the reservation.

"And then the whole annexation was nothing but a huge misunderstanding, well, at least partially." I ask what she means. "The most important reason that many voted in the referendum for affiliation with Russia was language. On the Crimean Peninsula, the majority of people speak Russian. But the Ukrainian government wanted to declare Ukrainian as the official language," she says. Meaning: all official documents would be drafted in Ukrainian. "But everyone thought that in the future they would end up in prison if they spoke Russian, which, of course, was never under consideration. Besides this, everyone saw the Russian propaganda promises: many tourists would come and people would be lining up to buy Crimean products." Higher pensions were announced. "They were actually implemented, only to be stopped exactly two months later."

Because of the sanctions, Alisa is not sure whether foreign credit cards are accepted in ATMs. She would like to try it out with mine. So we go to a cash dispenser in a small air-conditioned room, pleasantly refreshing after the heat outside. After the person ahead has withdrawn his money, I stick my card into the slot, switch languages to English, and punch in my PIN, but I get no further. A man with a buttoned-up shirt, plenty of muscles. and alcohol breath enters the room looking pretty upset and pushes me aside. He hammers at the screen until he eventually hits "cancel transaction." "Piss off, for fuck's sake, it's not your turn," he bellows, ripping my card out of the slot.

"Take it easy, we didn't notice the line," says Alisa, trying to calm the situation.

"Go on, piss off! Find someone else to con," the man barks. "We're not stupid, you're messing with the wrong guys."

He gets support from an older lady waiting behind him: "Can't you see there are other people waiting in line?" she yaps. No, unfortunately we must have overlooked them, Alisa explains, and asks why no one pointed out that there was a line. "We thought you were going to the desk, not withdrawing money. How much diopter do you have?" she asks, pointing at Alisa's glasses.

"Minus four," she answers

"Then you need stronger lenses!"

Would all the other people in the line hurl outrageous insults at us? Or would Mr. Universe decide that a good beating would be reasonable punishment for our offence? Leaning toward de-escalation, I resolve to make do with the ruble bills that I already have for another couple of days.

Truth No. 9:
Attempting to withdraw money with a foreign credit card in Crimea can lead to complications.

ABOUT A MILE away from the ancient site of Chersonesus we look out over Quarantine Bay and see warships heading to sea. Chersonesus, in its 2,500-year history, has been a military bastion, a trading base, and a place of exile. An event in 988 CE has ensured its place in Russian schoolbooks. In that year, Vladimir, the Grand Duke of Russia's precursor, Kievan Rus', was baptized here. Not because a cross had appeared in a dream or he had been won over by nightlong studies of the Bible. No, he called for tenders and asked emissaries of various world religions to examine which belief had the greatest potential to improve the lot of his country and unify it. The search for the true God as an assignment for McKinsey & Company, so to say. He allegedly eliminated Islam with the words: "Drinking is the joy of all Rus'. We cannot exist without that pleasure."[4]

He made the final decision, however, not only on the basis of his advisers' assessments but also because of his drive for power—and because of a woman. Vladimir was rather fond of Anna Porphyrogenita, sister of two Byzantine emperors. When Constantinople rejected his marriage proposal to her, he promptly seized Byzantine Chersonesus, threatened Constantinople with a similar fate, and renewed his request. Suddenly the Emperor was prepared to offer him Anna's hand in marriage, but with the proviso that he was baptized. Deal, said the Russian Grand Prince; Anna was dragged crying to the altar and the Kievan Rus' had a new state religion. To this day the Orthodox Church celebrates Vladimir as a saint.

At the site of his baptism, in the middle of ancient ruins, there is a white cathedral with a wide golden dome. "The Christians worship him, but actually he was very warlike," says Alisa. Right on cue a loud, muffled bang can be heard from the sea. Then another, and another. Is there gunfire coming from the bay? We go closer to the shore and see three warships leaving the harbor in three different directions. Large white numbers amidships help me to identify them later. They are the anti-submarine ship *Muromets* and two minesweepers, *Turbinist* and *Ivan Golubets*, both built in the 1970s. A small camouflaged pilot vessel patrols the entrance to the harbor, the blade slap of a military helicopter flying low above the archaeological site. "Choppers are a normal sight, but you seldom see so many ships at sea," says Alisa, and then with plenty of sarcasm in her voice adds, "Friendly little green ships." We couldn't find out what the bangs were, but none of the other Chersonesus visitors seem to be particularly disturbed, even though every now and then their eyes turn to the bay. Russian media report of increased military exercises due to the incident at the border;

it's probably something to do with that. Alisa is soon more interested in the flora around us than in the events in the bay. "Look, a pistachio tree!" she says. A little while later she identifies some clusters of arugula.

Three women are bathing on a sandy beach. We find a spot beneath a tree to shelter from the sun, which even in the afternoon is mercilessly hot. A couple of navy soldiers of the Black Sea Fleet moor a small motorboat by a seawall directly next to us. To celebrate the end of their working day they turn up their boom boxes so loud that half the bay can listen in, and sounds echo off the walls of St. Vladimir's Cathedral. Go, Russia! sings Oleg Gazmanov, a pop singer famous for extremely patriotic lyrics and videos, living proof that above-average success can be achieved with below-average talent.

> Russia, Russia,
> Fire and strength are in your name,
> Victory's flame is in your name!
> We raise the Russian flag!

echoes out across the bay. "Let's go," says Alisa.

"DO YOU REALLY believe Russia snatched Crimea because of the possibility of a tourist boom?" Konstantin asks me as we return to their village.

"Of course it was all about Sevastopol, the home port of the Black Sea Fleet. Putin's conduct toward Crimea reminds me of a backstreet mobster: if you see an expensive smartphone, just grab it." Konstantin has medium-length hair and a full beard and wears linen Ali Baba pants. The couple live with two daughters and a son, twelve, eight, and four years old, in a house they have mostly constructed themselves. A lot of wood, a wonderfully wild garden, and in every corner guitars, keyboards, drums, and flutes. The entire bathroom wall is painted with an image of a castle with a mermaid on its battlements; a hammock dangles from the roof truss. "We searched for three years for the perfect village," explains Konstantin. "It couldn't be too dirty, too poor, or have drunks on the street."

A B C
Grechka • ГРЕЧКА

The Russian word for buckwheat, a staple foodstuff that's an essential part of every breakfast for many people. At the end of 2014, when rumors were circulating that Western sanctions could lead to a shortage of buckwheat, there was panic-buying at the supermarkets, even though (or maybe because) the price of *grechka* was increasing rapidly. The fears were unfounded, but buckwheat is still considered a patriotic food as it isn't imported.

They found it right here, a little paradise near an idyllic lake, surrounded by forests and mountains. Most of the other villagers are Muslim Crimean Tatars. "For them we are new arrivals and almost like aliens," Konstantin says. "Opposite us there is a woman who practices Tibetan singing bowl therapy, and a couple of doors further, an author of esoteric books who holds spirit-channeling sessions on how to connect to light beings." He portions out a few pieces of nut cake. "And we have a 'mad professor' who invents various miracle machines. Steam treatment for back problems or short-wave therapy for activating the 'third eye.' And there's a meditation center." I get the feeling that I've ended up with the most normal "alien."

"Crimea has always attracted friends of alternative lifestyles because of its great nature, and because of its powerful places. Four years ago we organized a 'Rainbow Gathering' up in the mountains." The idea comes from the U.S., and since then there have been a number of offshoots. A couple of thousand visitors met in Crimea in a peaceful nature camp to spend their days with meditation, music, and marijuana.

Maybe it's a symbol of changing times that this week, a few miles away, the "Bike Show" of Putin's favorite motorbike gang, the Night Wolves, is taking place. *Do svidanya*, hippie dreamers; *privyet*, patriots in leather jackets. Since the crisis of 2014, during which a number of bikers roared through the Crimean Peninsula showing support for the separatists, they hold annual events in an abandoned industrial site near Sevastopol. The pompous shows, which are broadcast live on Russian TV and supported by funds from the Ministry of Culture in Moscow, seem like a mixture of a Rammstein concert, a *Mad Max*–inspired motorbike circus, and *Triumph of the Will*. The narrator is über–Night Wolf Alexander Zaldostanov, aka The Surgeon, a giant with despotic tendencies who loves stressing that he considers Stalin to be an idol and the West to be Satan. During the show, in the guttural tones of a baddie seldom found outside of kids' movies, he describes the battle between good (Russia) and evil (all kinds of "fascists") while heavy war machines roll across the stage. For the creators of this spectacle, there is no question that Crimea belongs to Russia and not Ukraine.

111

★

SHOOTING STARS

SASHA, A COUCHSURFER from Sevastopol, is also totally okay with the annexation. He implied this in his first email, writing in addition: "I'm looking forward to meeting a guest from the West again, I haven't had one for three years now." He suggests driving together to the observatory in Nauchnyj. On this August night a veritable downpour of shooting stars is expected.

We pack some muffins, chocolate bars, and Sasha's girlfriend, Anya, in his 1994 black BMW station wagon and drive north. Sasha is twenty-eight; as an engineer he invented a vacuum switch, as a hobby guitarist he composes heavy metal songs, and in his online profile he introduces himself as "rather conservative with old-fashioned views."

"Ukraine has always been divided, since 1991," he says. "In every election you could see a clear difference between east and west, between the Russian and the Ukrainian parts." What he always disapproved of was the hero-worshipping of Nazi collaborators in Ukraine. "Every year they celebrate the foundation of the Galician Division—they were volunteers affiliated to the ss. I think it's wrong; my grandpa was in the Red Army." He goes on to speak about fears of prohibiting the Russian language and the chaotic acts of the Ukrainian leaders. "When the 'polite soldiers' started to pop up in Sevastopol my only thought was—at last they are coming to support us."

Many Russians don't understand why the acquisition of Crimea caused such an international outcry. After all, there was a referendum, with the majority voting for attachment to Russia. In Western media reports there really were some details that were given short shrift; for instance, the fears surrounding the dismissal of the Ukrainian President Viktor Yanukovych in February 2014. When the Maiden protesters were celebrating their success, many were worried that this was just the beginning of an extremely anti-Russian backlash, particularly as the future role of the far-right nationalist party the Right Sector—who were involved in the protests—was unclear. There also was a lot of skepticism about an association agreement with the EU, which excluded a close economic partnership with Russia.

That was the situation when the "little green men" suddenly started appearing in Crimea. The Russian propaganda machinery stoked existing prejudices with its typical exaggeration and the referendum was arranged in a rush to capture the mood of the moment.

But it's also clear that the results of the referendum were embellished, as shown by the investigations of Moscow's Centre for Analysis of Strategies and Technologies. The voter turnout and the secessionists' lead were both lower than originally claimed. And the deployment of Russian soldiers on Ukrainian territory was against international law, regardless of how polite they were and even if no bullet was fired in Crimea.

We reach the grounds of the observatory, a park between research stations capped with white domes housing huge telescopes. Sasha walks straight past them and directly toward a clearing, where dozens of other onlookers have already gathered. It's a clear night and here, some two thousand feet above sea level, the visibility is particularly good.

A B C
H
—

A letter that in Cyrillic is pronounced as an *N*; our familiar *H* sound doesn't exist at all. As a substitute Г, the equivalent of our *G*, is mostly used for foreign words, thus giving us names like Dashiell Gammet, Gunter S. Thompson, German Gesse, and Adolf Gitler as well as cities like Galifax, Gonolulu, and Gouston. Sometimes, however, the Arabic *H* becomes a Cyrillic *X* (pronounced "ch"), as in David Chasselchoff or Chulk Chogan.

We spread a blanket and lie next to one another on our backs. Sasha has a night sky app and looks for Perseus; the greatest spectacle is expected in the environs of this constellation. Very soon Anya sees the first shooting star; a short while later Sasha and I also see one. Every now and then you can hear oohs and aahs as other people see a spot of light moving across the sky.

"What's your wish?" I ask them both.

"I'm actually quite satisfied with my life," says Sasha. "I like being an engineer; even as a kid I used to build incredible things with Lego. Okay, a guitar maker would also be a pretty cool job."

"I would love to earn more money," says Anya, who works for the city administration. "We have become poorer since belonging to Russia because the ruble is so low." She begins humming the melody of 'Dream a Little Dream of Me."

At three-minute intervals, shooting stars streak across the firmament like tiny, incandescent satellites. We eat crumbly chocolate muffins, staring up at the heavens. "My grandma was always talking about Yuri Gagarin," says Anya. "How the whole country partied when he became the first man in space. Will we ever experience such a moment of pride?"

Sasha asks himself the same question. His generation is missing any higher ideals, he says. "What does Europe stand for?" he wants to know.

For an absurd administrative apparatus that no one understands and lots of bureaucracy, I think. "For peace," I say, which is also true. In the movie version of our conversation there would be a cut to a particularly bright shooting star. Return question. "What does Russia stand for?"

"If I only knew," says Sasha. "Our grandparents had the war. Our parents had Communism. They both had ideals, something that gave their lives meaning. But what have we got?"

IT IS PRECISELY this vacuum that made the reacquisition of Crimea so emotional for many Russians. After March of 2014, Putin's approval ratings skyrocketed, as did the sales figures of "Our Crimea" fridge magnets.

For many it was the country's proudest moment in a quarter of a century. Not least because the President had demonstrated that he was capable of standing up to the West,

115

the same West that had time and again humiliated Russia (even though most people in the West hadn't realized it). From the expansion of NATO to the east, which was perceived as an aggressive encroachment and a breach of promise, to Barack Obama's remark that Russia was no more than a "regional power" (which was more painful than Ronald Reagan's "evil empire," a label that at least demonstrated some respect). Offended national pride is possibly a more important factor in the current escalation of the crisis between East and West than most people realize. And Putin knows he can bank on the patriotism of his countrymen, particularly at a time when the economy is faltering.

In 2016, pollsters from the Levada Center asked Russians what made them particularly proud of their country. The most frequently mentioned points were: history, natural resources, the military, culture, and the size of the country. At the end of the scale were the health and school systems and economic development; the category "fellow citizens" was also notice-ably low on the list. Interestingly, in comparison to previous surveys, there was a steep decline in admiration for Russia's success in sports, which was certainly linked to the doping dis-closures. The military made the largest leap up the ladder.

I always find it a bit strange when pride is directed toward something that has nothing to do with one's own achievements. But during my travels here I discovered two variants of this that I can understand. One is a great enthusiasm for the Russian language, which is considered pretty difficult, so those who can master it are justifiably proud. The other is an appreciation of being able to cope with the difficult conditions that often come with living in Russia. An if-you-can-make-it-here-you-can-make-it-anywhere kind of pride, rather like a doctor in a crisis zone, a teacher in a high-needs school, or an Antarctic researcher.

YALTA HAS TWO partner cities in Europe: Nice in France and Baden-Baden in Germany. With the first it shares an extensive seaside esplanade, with the second a longstanding affection among spa visitors (although Baden-Baden can't boast of a monumental building like the Druzhba Sanatorium. In the 1980s, its unusual UFO shape and honeycomb windows made the U.S. Secret Service believe it might be a launching pad for rockets.)

Here there is little evidence of the tension of recent times. Tourists stroll around, the cafés and fast food stores are well attended, the boulevards have an all-the-fun-of-the-fair vibe. Until, suddenly, the heavens darken and a heavy summer shower begins flooding the streets. In the pedestrian zone, I seek shelter with others under an awning. It's so crowded that striking up conversation is unavoidable. The women next to me are called Masha and Natasha and are former tournament-level synchronized swimmers (I'm not making this up). "How could you do that if you're afraid of water?" I ask, pointing at the dark sky. They find it so funny that they invite me to join them in the Grand Café at the next corner, where we wait for the weather to improve. We eat heart-shaped raspberry cakes and drink heart-colored fruit infusions while a projector beams City-of-Love scenes of Paris onto the wall. We talk shop about water acrobatics and book writing and Masha enthuses about the best wine bars in Paris, where she currently lives. Both of them stress that Crimea belongs to Russia, which they feel duty-bound to tell me as a foreigner. The weather front moves on, so we say our farewells and wade off in different directions; the streets have transformed into torrents.

I am exuberantly greeted in a sushi bar; the owner hasn't seen tourists other than Russians and Ukrainians for years. "Are you enjoying yourself? You're traveling alone? That's possible? You're very brave!" I feel a bit like an exotic animal, but I also feel the hope from people here that soon there will be more non-Russian visitors.

FLIRTING FOR PROS

AT SIMFEROPOL AIRPORT the most beautiful woman I've seen in all my travels here is waiting at Gate B6. Mid-twenties, intelligent dark eyes, face like a young Mila Kunis, skin vacation-tanned. The innocence of her knee-length, floral-patterned summer dress contrasts with the wackiness of her four-inch-high platform sandals. Sitting upright, graceful and proud among the dozens of squatting, hunched travelers waiting for announcements, she stands out like a peacock butterfly amid bark beetles.

As experienced womanizers know, when flirting with a celestial beauty there is one thing to keep in mind: these sublime creatures are so often spoken to, smiled at, and attempted to be picked up that one has to find a more unusual tactic— which, owing to the effect of surprise, will remain indelibly anchored in her mind.

I take a free seat six feet away from her; between us there is a gap in the seating and two sockets, one of which she is using to charge her cell phone. And then I ignore her. I ignore her in the most exquisite ways, tapping away on my cell phone, rummaging around in my backpack, checking my flight info, always careful to project an uncomplicated, confident body language. Nonchalantly pulling my passport out of my outdoor-pursuit backpack and browsing through the visa pages, I am signaling: here is a man who knows precisely what he is doing.

She must then ask herself why this aloof, fragrant (Calvin Klein One on the left wrist, Acqua di Giò on the right wrist—I had just come from Duty Free) man in hiking shoes is paying her no attention whatsoever. From the corner of my eye I observe my success: she runs her fingers through her hair a couple of times, once curling a lock around one of her fingers, an unmistakable sign that she's considering her options.

From a leather designer handbag she takes out a large bottle of Lipton Ice Tea, which I pay no attention to, just as I pay no attention to the delicate tossing back of her head and the almost-caressing contact between plastic and mouth. An ad featuring this scene would triple Lipton's profits within days.

Now I have four options:

OPTION 1: "Oh, wow! Is that *really* lemon ice tea? I desperately need some! Where did you buy it?"

OPTION 2: "Yuck! Lemon ice tea! Peach is much better!"

OPTION 3: "Did you know that Cleopatra regularly bathed in lemon ice tea?"

OPTION 4: Continue to ignore. I'm a pro, so of course I select that one.

She disconnects her cell phone from the socket, which I pay no attention to, not even with a glance, and begins to compose some messages. In doing so her face shows not a single sign of emotion, which could have something to do with the fact that her digital conversation isn't that interesting and instead she's considering how to start up a conversation with the mysterious stranger sitting next to her without appearing too brash. Who knows the internal turmoil she must be going through this evening at Gate B6 of Simferopol Airport? Well, a bit of suffering is part of the game. So, I tap away at my cell phone with a smile on my face, signaling to her that even at a long distance with WhatsApp I lead a fulfilling social life with my hipster circle of friends, all great-looking, successful people.

She reconnects to the socket; I plug my ebook reader in the socket next to hers. I open up a digital version of Chekhov's *The Cherry Orchard*, indicating high intellect. There is such strong symbolism in our electronic devices recharging next to each other that I unavoidably envision us together in 2025, driving our new generation Lada to gather up our gorgeous twins, Masha and Natasha, from their synchronized swimming lessons.

But it's still important to continue ignoring. The complicated alpha-female psyche will punish premature directness with a loss of interest. The ensuing minutes of sitting in silence next to each other will give her synapses time to develop an explosive mixture of attraction and insecurity that she will inevitably interpret as being in love.

After half an hour she gathers her phone and handbag and disappears toward the washroom. There are hardly any free seats and a couple with a small kid seize the opportunity and take her seat. The kid whines.

Five minutes later the mother-to be of our twins reappears, appraises the situation (surely cursing under her breath, but with enough class that no one notices), and remains standing in the hall fifty feet away. She and her cell phone and her bottle of ice tea. I pay no attention, but I'm jealous of those two items.

The flight is called at Gate B4. Fortuna and Cupid have come to an agreement and decided that we are to have the same destination, as I notice in the cagelike waiting room into which passengers have been crammed to have their tickets inspected. I position myself ten feet away from her. Coquettishly, she appears not to notice me and plays with a strand of her hair.

Fortuna has prepared another surprise for us. The lady is sitting in 11D and I'm in 12C, places diagonally opposite each other, making it easy for me to continue not paying attention to her. She unpacks her white headphones and watches *The Hunger Games* on her cell. Only a thriller about life and death can distract her from her inner emotional chaos.

I lose her at the luggage collection at Saint Petersburg when my backpack takes longer than her black trolley bag. I totally ignore how gracefully she walks toward the exit. As consolation, at least I know that the memory of this encounter, all those nagging what-ifs, will occupy her mind for years to come. No doubt about that.

VODKA
CURES ALL

WHEN THE BAND Leningrad recorded their song "V Pitere Pit'" (In Saint Petersburg, you drink) they probably expected a number of different reactions: indignation from the citizens of Saint Petersburg, trouble with the law, criticism from the Ministry of Health. And they got all of these in no short supply, but there were also two surprises. First, the mind-boggling popularity of the song, which in no time had amassed two million hits on YouTube. And second, praise from the Saint Petersburg Committee for Tourist Development: "The song triggers an urge to discover for yourself everything that can be seen here—monuments, museums, restaurants, events, festivals for all tastes and age groups," claimed its director, Viktor Kononov.

His remarks are all the more extraordinary as monuments and museums play no role whatsoever in the lively ska-pop song. The song's message can be summed up thus: in Moscow people sniff cocaine, in Rostov they smoke pot, but true drinkers are found in "Piter," as the locals endearingly refer to their city. In the music video you can see employees from a variety of businesses telling their bosses how they really feel about them, leaving their workplaces, and then getting totally wasted. Vodka acts as a cure-all for every life circumstance; it would have been less surprising if the distilling industry rather than the tourist officials had used "V Pitere Pit'" for its purposes.

My hostess, Arina, visibly enjoys translating the lyrics while we knock back massive amounts of Georgian red wine. The song in all its coarseness is a subversive masterpiece, especially since Saint Petersburg is considered the intellectual capital of the country, a metropolis so permeated with high culture that the local pizza service is called "Dostoyevsky" and afternoon tea is referred to in the local slang as "Tchaikovsky" instead of chai. Arina has long blond hair, is roughly five foot nine, and is one of those people who with every confident gesture, casual expletive, and drag on a cigarette seem more rock star–like than most real rock stars. Her online profile includes a photo of her holding a sign like a beggar that reads: "I'm from Russia. I sell drugs, weapons, and child pornography" and another photo with the caption: "My father is a bear and my mother a balalaika." When I saw her profile I thought: *This will be interesting.*

She lives at the southern tip of Saint Petersburg in a high-rise not far from the Gazprom headquarters, a few bus stops on from the last subway station at Prospekt Veteranov. Her bookshelf contains Kurt Vonnegut, "German Gesse," Murakami, Sartre, Pelevin, and illustrated books on street art. Next to the bookshelf is a heap of VIP passes for concerts and conventions—she works as an event manager.

At home Arina looks after two cats, Misha and Masha, both strong characters. Time and again she breaks off mid-sentence with a "Miiissshhhaaa. Tsk tsk tsk!" or a "Marusya! What are you doing??!!" directed at the creatures.

Three-month-old Masha, nicknamed Marusya, is at the moment not quite compos mentis, as she has licked up drops of wine from the floor. Since then she has been trying out ridiculous climbing maneuvers on the kitchen curtains without ever reaching her target, the windowsill. In "Piter" even the cats drink.

Arina is an expert on Russian rock music. She plays me her favorite songs from Saint Petersburg groups like Splean, Kino, The Night Snipers, and Leningrad at volumes that the neighbors probably find a bit excessive.

She tells me that the last time she had a journalist as a guest there was a bit of trouble with the Federal Security Service (FSB). "An Indian sport photographer. At the airport he was immediately intercepted and questioned because he had a press card. The agents wanted to know what he was doing here and how long he was planning to stay. He was nervous and gave them my telephone number." A telephone call from the FSB didn't fluster Arina, however, as she'd had plenty of dealings with the security agency through her job. Once a year she works for the Saint Petersburg Economic Forum, which President Putin also attends. "Sometimes in the week before the event they tap into my phone. I know when it's happening as the phone gets hot and my battery drains quickly."

So she picked up the phone and the FSB agent wanted to know her connection to the Indian man. She assured the agent that her guest wasn't a terrorist and said to let him go. Then the agent asked for her address. "I said: Excuse me, are you really from the FSB? We've been talking for five minutes and you haven't checked my phone number and found my address?" The tipsy cat jumps onto Arina's lap and she laughs hoarsely. "The guy got mad: 'Do you know who you're speaking to? I work for the FSB!' And me: 'So what?' He: 'Federal. Security. Service.' And I just said: 'We talk and talk and you still don't know where I am? Are you an intern or what?'"

After a slight delay the Indian guest appeared at her door. He seemed to be pretty wired and right away asked what the hell she had done: immediately after the telephone call the FSB had told him he could gather his stuff and go.

"First of all, I said: 'Sit down. Next month I have an event for the United Nations. If I have any kind of trouble with the FSB, believe me: I'll find you. I know India is big. But I will find you.'" The poor man didn't get off to a good start in Saint Petersburg, but after a few drinks he managed to calm himself down a bit.

Arina says many of her friends think it's strange that she, as a woman living alone, takes on couchsurfing guests. She begins playing around with a switchblade with great skill.

"They ask me whether I'm afraid. Of rape and such things. I have this knife: once across the forehead and you can't see for the blood. Once through the hollow of the knee or along the inside of the elbow and you can't move." She puts the weapon aside, cracks her knuckles, and rummages the next Winston out of the pack. "Want one?"

A B C

Itchiness • ЗУД

In superstitious Russia, a sign of the near future, with your fortune depending on the body part affected. The nose: An impending drinking session. The soles of the feet: A journey is in the cards. Lips: You will soon be kissed. Left hand: Money is on the way. Right hand: You will soon meet a friend. Right eye: Tears are coming up. Left eye: You have reasons to be cheerful. Throat: A celebration is approaching. Or there's going to be a fight. Or both. And if everything itches at the same time: Go to a doctor.

Discreetly trying to change the topic, I ask her why she has a sign on the kitchen wall that says "I don't want to work" in German. Arina says she finds German a melodious language. She even had a Nietzsche quotation tattooed on her back: "You need chaos in your soul to give birth to a dancing star." She read *Thus Spoke Zarathustra* for the first time when she was fourteen and it has influenced her to this day.

127

She is astonished as I tell her that many of my fellow Germans are not so enthusiastic about the sound of their mother tongue. "You mean like in those videos with 'butterfly' and 'science'?" She is referring to the popular YouTube series *German Versus Other Languages*, where people from different countries pronounce various words. At the end there's always a German wearing a traditional hat, with a stein of wheat beer in front of him and the harsh tone of a sergeant major, as though he's spitting out the words:

"*Papillon*."

"*Butterfly*."

"*Farfalla*."

"*Mariposa*."

"SCHMETTTERRRLING!"

The Russian language can be both *mariposa* and *Schmetterling*, as Arina demonstrates with two ad-lib renditions of poems. The first sounds soft and cajoling ("Shagane, Oh My, Shagane" by Sergei Yesenin), the second hard and staccato ("And Could You?" by Vladimir Mayakovsky).

Russian sounds meanest in the vernacular known as *mat*, which is extensively used by Leningrad, the band mentioned earlier. I get a small but intensive course from Arina, the contents of which I won't repeat here word for word in deference to sensitive Russian readers. As my teacher was highly skilled in graphically describing the right situation for using each word, here, at least, is a short extract: "Imagine a friend calls you up and asks you whether you can remember the incredibly ugly girl at the last party. You say, sure, and he says 'I got her pregnant.' The only possible reply is '*Pizdets!*'" The word means something like "catastrophe" or "wow, fucked up" but is derived from a vulgar term for a woman's sexual organ.

For people who want who want to become more familiar with this linguistically not uninteresting universe of curses, I can recommend the Wikipedia entry "Mat (Russian profanity)." Here, we continue with castles and ballet.

Truth No. 10:
The Russian word for butterfly is babochka.

★

CITY OF BOOKS

THE SUBWAY TRAIN on Line I is completely adorned with books. As advertising for a literary festival, the illustrations on the car exteriors recreate the major attractions of the city using books: the Hermitage Museum, Kazan Cathedral, the Bronze Horseman. Inside the train, I get the impression that more people here read novels on paper to pass the time than in any other subway in the world. The number of smartphone typists and book readers seem to balance out.

At each stop the doors rumble open, passengers get off and on, and the distorted station announcements crackle over the internal loudspeakers. Some static humming is followed by a sudden moment of silence, as if the power has been cut, and for a second absolutely nothing happens. Two point eight million passengers experience this unusual moment of silence at every stop, every day. This short pause in the conveyor belt–like passenger transportation system deep below Europe's fourth-largest megacity is so pleasant that once you've experienced it, you almost yearn for it during the ride.

From the stop at Nevsky Prospect I walk along a six-lane road of the same name toward the west. "Once you step onto the Prospect you immediately sense a certain fragrance of cheerful idleness," wrote Nikolai Gogol 180 years ago, and this still applies today. "Even if you had important business, you'd probably forget it as soon as you stepped into the street."[5]

The fragrance of idleness smells best in the spectacular Art Nouveau building of the delicatessen Yeliseev's Food Hall, a paradise for fans of French pralines, caviar, and champagne. For the time being, however, you have to be a little careful at the cheese counter. Since the sanctions were enforced after the Crimean crisis, Russia, as a countermeasure, placed a ban on cheese from Europe. So the opulent displays of Terra del Gusto gorgonzola or Schönfeld Blue turn out to be not fine products of Italian or German cheese-makers, but Russian imitations at pretty high prices.

There are noticeably many tourists from China; for several years now, ever-increasing numbers have been visiting Russia. In the Polyanka souvenir shop, a busload of Far Easterners stock up on a busload of matryoshka dolls, while in the shop window, mechanical wooden bears with balalaikas get into the groove. Here, too, Gogol was right. "Peer less at the shop windows: the knickknacks displayed in them are beautiful but they smell of a terrible quantity of banknotes."[6] At the end of his short story, rapture turns to disgust as the narrator concludes that everything on Nevsky Prospect is but lies and deception. For him the two-and-a-half-mile-long grand boulevard is a stage for all the facets of human falsity, a place where nothing is as it seems. At least as far as the cheese is concerned I have to agree with him.

I reach the Hermitage Museum, with its green-golden facade. In front of the building are groups with guides holding signs in the air displaying the names of cruise lines: Pullmantur 7, MCS 3, Pullmantur 14, Volga Dream 4. But for today, I skip Michelangelo's *Crouching Boy* and Caravaggio's *Lute-Player* and instead carry on along the banks of the Neva, on the other side of the museum. In front of a hydrofoil called *Meteor 182*, which looks like something out of a 1960s sci-fi movie, I meet up with Anna. I contacted her a few weeks previously by email and she promised to show me her two favorite places.

A B C

Jokes • шутки

Russian humor has long featured a set of archetypal characters that are known to everyone: Poruchik Rzhevsky, a rude cavalry officer; Rabinovich, a cynical Russian Jew; and Vovochka, the equivalent of "Little Johnny"—a plain-speaking small boy. In the '90s, another character was added to the list: the "New Russian," a poorly educated, arrogant businessman who drives a black Mercedes s600 car and got rich under dubious circumstances. Example: The son of a New Russian complains to his father, "Everyone in my class takes the bus to school. I feel like a misfit in my Mercedes 600." The dad replies: "Don't worry, I'll buy you a bus; then you can go to school like everyone else!"

The waters of the Neva, the color of a sage lozenge, glisten like foil on the way to the Gulf of Finland; the clouds have the matte hue of old silver. "The most beautiful thing about Saint Petersburg is the sky," says Anna. "Every day it is different, every imaginable shade of gray. Sometimes there are purple tones in it, sometimes more yellowish. When I leave the office in the afternoon, I often simply look up and enjoy the beauty."

She works on the administrative side of a pharmaceutical company, is twenty-nine, and wears a black leather jacket over a black dress, with a black handbag, black tights, and black shoes. For balance she has blond hair and a white cell phone, which is always in her hands. Her eyes resemble an evening sky in Saint Petersburg in fall—melancholic blue-gray.

"For me this sea symbolizes freedom; it's like the waiting room to the world of the gods," she says half an hour later as we dock at Peterhof Palace. A pier, a wild natural coastline, cliffs, and dark sand. Anna teaches me the meaning of the word *chandra*, a kind of weltschmerz, or noble melancholy. This is the perfect place for it. "You're feeling good, you have everything you need, but you're tired from being happy, tired from all this carefreeness, you need a rest," is how she describes the feeling. "*Chandra* is an important part of the Russian soul."

The view of the sea reminds me of an episode of the Russian cartoon series *Masyanya*. The main character, a neurotic twentysomething philosopher, sits in front of her TV, depressed, and says, "How bad everything is. War everywhere, death, stupidity. And what do we do? Just drink." Then she gets on her bike, rides to the seaside, sings a sad song out of tune, and the blues vanish. The sea helps; maybe "V Pitere Pit'" isn't the only solution to problems.

On the grounds of Peterhof Palace a few yards inland, every hedge is clipped, every grassy area mown; gilded sculptures glow as if in competition with the freshly painted palace

133

facade. It feels as if the czar has just popped down to the pub for a quick drink and could be back at any moment.

A good three hundred years ago Peter the Great broke from the traditions of his predecessors in many ways. He traveled extensively through Europe, commissioned Russia's first warship, and moved the capital from Moscow to Saint Petersburg, although the swampy land to the north made the building work a grind. Sometimes he was a little overzealous with his reforms; for instance, he allowed his subjects to grow beards only if they paid a beard tax. He had Peterhof Palace built as a summer residence; the extensions were added by a number of his successors, but mostly by Czarina Elizabeth, a Baroque fan. During World War II, the Germans caused appalling damage here, and then Stalin had the city bombed to prevent the Nazis from using its rich symbolism for victory celebrations. In the meantime, most of the buildings have been reconstructed to be true to the originals.

Palaces, fountains, and sculptures: the typical requisites of rulers, as found at Versailles or Sanssouci. But no other palace in the world offers the Peterhof mixture of sea-view *chandra* and rascally humor: to wit, there are booby traps for visitors here. You'll be sitting peacefully on a bench and suddenly a jet of water comes at you. Even sauntering down what seems to be an innocent-looking pathway you can become unexpectedly wet. You have to imagine Peter was a mischievous czar.

Anna's favorite fountain is free of trickery, a cascade some sixty feet long with four steplike plateaus made of chessboard-patterned marble; right at the top there are three fearsome green water-spitting dragons. "It's good to know that some things don't change," she says. "When I was a kid I was happiest here, and that's still true today." Behind the dragons there

Arrival in Moscow. My ten-week journey through Russia began in the capital.

The monument at the vdnkh. Many Russians still remember the pioneering feats of the cosmonauts with pride.

At the Revolution Square subway station. The snout of this dog statue has been stroked to a high polish.

Underground palaces. The Moscow subway network was a prestige
project for Stalin.

My host Genrich. His online profile was off-putting, but he turned out to
be a warm and intelligent host.

The cost of rebuilding the Chechen capital, Grozny, ran to many billions of dollars. In many places there are no longer any signs of the war.

Encounters in Ingushetia. The handling of children and weapons takes some getting used to—I was greeted on several occasions with a gun salute.

The mosque in Argun. I was surprised to hear German music coming from the guard's cell phone.

From Heart to Heart, the poster reads. Images of the powers that be are ever-present.

Couchsurfing in North Caucasus. The tables are particularly lavish for fast breaking at the end of Ramadan.

Autocrat on the rear windshield. The governor, Ramzan Kadyrov, is a master of self-promotion.

"There's more to eat next door." People's hospitality was most impressive.

At home with Renat in Makhachkala. The thirty-seven-year-old spoke in a wonderful mixture of English and German.

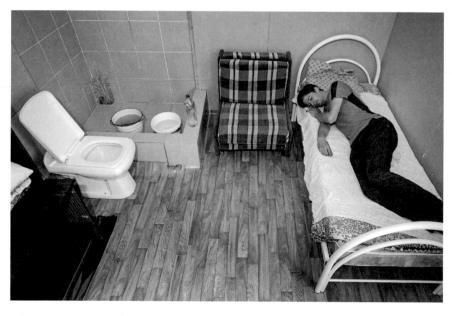

His guest room took a bit of getting used to, but the bed was very comfortable.

We were met by these friendly gentlemen in the village center of Balkhar, in the mountains of Dagestan.

Ghost town with images of Stalin. In Shukty, two hundred luxury houses were planned to be built but never finished.

Tibet? Bhutan? Japan? None of the above: this Buddhist temple can be found in Europe, namely in the city of Elista.

I stayed three days with Sergei (left) in Volgograd, where I met two other couchsurfers, David and Natalia.

In Crimea, I watched warships in Quarantine Bay, near Sevastopol.

The promenade at Yalta. Tourists are slowly returning here; visitors from Western Europe, however, are extremely rare.

Sweet-tasting Yalta onions only grow in Crimea; these ones were on display at the market in Sevastopol.

I spent some very happy days in a small village with Alisa, Konstantin, and their three children.

Many locals complain about rising prices in Crimea since the reintroduction of the ruble.

In many of the larger cities there are "time cafés" like this one in Saint Petersburg. Guests pay for the time they spend there, not what they consume.

Saint Petersburg from above. Every day the sky is different, but the city is always enveloped in its own special melancholy.

Tourists not prone to vertigo can get a good view from a rooftop tour.

Golden grandeur. Peterhof Palace is one of the best-known attractions in the area; the playful water features show that the czars had a sense of humor.

A fishmonger in Makhachkala. At the market you can also buy illegally fished sturgeon, famed for its meat and as a supplier of caviar.

is a closed wooden door set into an angular stone wall. "When I was young, I was convinced that dwarves lived there. Kids nowadays are too clever, they don't believe such things." .

THE EVENING, BACK in the city, is dedicated to another of Anna's childhood memories. As a seven-year-old, she saw *Swan Lake* for the first time in the Mariinsky Theatre. Posters in front of the foyer boast that the world-famous theater is running its 234th season this year. Maybe Czar and Czarina didn't go to the pub but slipped out of Peterhof for an evening of culture.

The auditorium has hardly changed over the years. Painted cherubs on the ceiling dance around the huge chandelier; the golden balconies have creaky wooden floors.

What unfolds on the stage over the next three hours evokes impressions you'll rarely find in news stories about Russia: airiness, beauty, and elegance. The music is cozy, creating a feeling of euphoria that calms the soul. Movement and

135

sound harmonize completely. All around us, people begin to sob quietly when Odette and the Prince dance at the end of the second act without noticing that the evil sorcerer, Rothbart, is watching them. "*That* is the Russian soul: melancholy and beauty," Anna whispers to me, rummaging in her handbag for tissues.

That was easy. There are supposedly people who have spent decades searching for this elusive Russian soul. And all the time the shy thing was hiding in the Mariinsky, maybe in a crease in the curtain or under a loose plank in the orchestra pit. Lonely, hidden, always on the run from the cleaning ladies or stagehands, and always waiting until the end of the second act of *Swan Lake* to quickly dash onto the stage.

YELTSIN

FROM A GEOGRAPHICAL viewpoint Europe ends at the Ural Mountain range, 870 miles east of Moscow and some 25 miles from Yekaterinburg. So a whole lot of Russia is part of Europe, and yet we normally only think of the Balkan states, Romania, and Poland when we speak of Eastern Europe. Among geographers the eastern border is contentious; for the locals it's fairly irrelevant, as the whole Ural region was always considered Russian.

Europe. In Russia's history the "old continent" was time and again an object of comparison. Sometimes as model and yardstick, sometimes as competitor that needed to be outdone. In the recent past, within a very short period of time, attitudes toward Europe have changed drastically, according to Lev Gudkov, director of the prestigious sociological research organization Levada. While in 1991, 71 percent of Russians considered themselves European, by 2008 the figure was only 21 percent. And after the Crimean crisis, Russia's relationship to the West and identification with its values reached rock bottom. We should drop the illusion that Russia wants to head toward "Westernization," which some people believe is almost a predetermined natural law when a nondemocratic system collapses. Russia is seeking its own way.

I have spoken to many Russians about Europe and was surprised by some of their observations. I never had the impression of living in the midst of a dynamic entity on its way to reinventing itself, but many Euroskeptic Russians perceive a great deal of recent change: a shift away from traditional values like family ("Help! Homosexuals!") and from their own culture ("Help! Muslim refugees!"). Besides that, some regard Europe as an ice-cold power construct without morals or passion which, despite its own lapses, has a strong tendency to lecture others in the name of humanity. Many people disapprove of the close links between Europe and the U.S.; some greatly overestimate America's influence. "Is it true that Angela Merkel gets her orders directly from the White House?" one host asked me. A number of times I was invited simply to move to Volgograd or Novosibirsk to escape the life-threatening refugee crisis in Europe. People in the simplest of mini-apartments, living on US$230 a month and not knowing if they would have hot water the next day, felt sorry for me because of my background. Because they know from their TVs how bad things apparently are in Germany.

The days of Europe euphoria in the early 1990s seem an eternity ago. But not in Yekaterinburg's Yeltsin Museum, in the Yeltsin Center on Yeltsin Street. Russia's first democratically elected president spent the majority of his life in the country's fourth-largest city. That's why they erected this museum on the banks of the Iset as a monument to him, costing hundreds of millions of dollars. The sievelike walls and

138

huge window facade signal transparency. From the square in front of the building, you can see the dome of the Church of the Savior on Spilled Blood, on the opposite side of the river. It's located on the site of the murder of the last czar, Nicholas II, and his entire family, in July of 1918. Only a little over a mile as the crow flies separates a monument to the beginning of Communist rule from a monument to its demise.

The tour of the museum begins in a movie theater. A technically elaborately produced, wide-screen animated film condenses a thousand years of Russian history into eight minutes. From Ivan the Terrible to Nicholas II, from Peter the Great to Brezhnev, almost all of the rulers look like boss villains from video games. A female voice speaks of the dark times of Stalin's Great Purge, when "ten to twenty million people died." Toward the end you see Gorbachev in a crane

139

with a wrecking ball, because he came to the conclusion that if you "couldn't improve or reform the system, then it has to be destroyed." The final image shows the ten most important rulers from the past gathered together; Yeltsin is at the far right of the line at "the beginning of the history of a new, free Russia."

The video is remarkable because it doesn't relativize the many gruesome acts of history, unlike the typical Russian history books. The economic advances under Stalin remain unmentioned and Lenin is depicted as a deceiver, promising the people a brighter future but leading them into an era of fear and violence.

Conservative commentators reacted pretty angrily to these eight minutes of scary cinema. The accusations went as far as suggesting that American propagandists were behind the whole thing. Critics considered it absurd to allow school classes into this showing. A version of the video available online was only "liked" 70 times but had more than 750 thumbs down.

Sure enough the exhibition glorifies Yeltsin as a saint, although in a pretty entertaining way. Like the Seven Days of Creation, the seven most important days in the political life of the president are depicted in photos and film documents, with voiceovers from comrades and experts. A historian states that Yeltsin himself admitted it was a mistake to start the Chechen War, but that history later proved his decision was right. Gradually a picture emerges of a statesman who in the most difficult times made forward-looking (and somehow always correct) choices. As proof, every visitor can take home a copy of the constitution, which took effect after a referendum toward the end of 1993. A young red-haired museum guest gets pretty upset as she reads through the various points. "'No one should be forced to follow an ideology'? It happens. 'Free university education'? Not true. 'Freedom of expression'? No. 'Sexual liberty'? 'Equal rights for men and women'? Also no!" Today's realities do not live up to these ideals.

A B C
Kiselyov, Dmitry • КИСЕЛЁВ, ДМИТРИЙ

Head of the government-owned news agency Rossiya Segodnya, and often termed the Kremlin's chief propagandist. While Americans might settle down on Sunday evenings in front of a crime show on TV, at the same time in Russia, on Kiselyov's program *Vesti Nedeli* ("News of the Week"), the crime is always Western politics. As a host, Kiselyov enjoys being provocative, sometimes hitting the wrong note: once he compared Obama to an ape; another time he compared Putin to Stalin (and he meant it in a positive sense); and once he proudly announced that Russia was "the only country that could turn America into radioactive ash."

The walk-in exhibits, which include a trolley bus (Yeltsin was a man of the people and sometimes used public transport) and a food store from the crisis times of the '90s, are particularly evocative. There are only two types of goods on offer—a pyramid of canned seaweed salad and Mason jars of pear juice.

The room marked "Day seven" contains an exact replica of the leader's office. A jacket hangs above the leather seat, four telephones sit in an orderly row, and the dominant colors are beige and light green, against which the tinseled Christmas tree fits in perfectly. All Russians recognize this office and tree from a historic TV moment on December 31, 1999. That was when the agitated president, breathing deeply, announced his resignation. On the seventh day God ended his work, so to say. He had done what he could; now it was time for a younger successor. He apologized for the things he hadn't managed to do, declared Vladimir Putin interim president and the best candidate for the forthcoming elections in March, and ended by saying: "Be happy. You deserve happiness and peace. Happy New Year. Happy New Century, my dear people."

NEWS AND
NARRATIVES

YELTSIN TALKED ABOUT happiness and peace, and both can be found in Siberia by just glancing out the train window at the sheer endless forests. During the journey there's plenty of time for reflection: the 076Э to Novosibirsk takes twenty-two hours. I lie on the bed in the coach and observe what's happening around me. An elderly gentleman in colorful shorts and polished leather shoes nibbles at some *sushki* cookies, which he's eating with his pot noodles; two small children are comparing belly buttons and come to the conclusion that they're both really funny. Once I've had my fill of landscape and people, I catch up on some news.

From *Sputnik* I learn something unsettling: "German Federal Government prepares citizens for war—Media" is the headline of one article. Have I missed something on my travels? I carry on reading and realize that the headline was misleading. It was referring to a report in the *Frankfurter Allgemeine Sonntagszeitung* about a government plan for recommendations to citizens in the event of a crisis, which involves stocking up on food and water at home. However, in the sixth paragraph, *Sputnik* quotes from the document: "An attack on German territory requiring conventional national defense is unlikely."

The article is technically true; it's just that the verb "prepare" in the headline suggests a different story. Soccer players prepare themselves for the World Championships; schoolkids prepare for exams. So normally it describes things that are sure or highly likely to happen. Such subtleties are important, as many readers just scroll through the headlines.

If you regularly read the news through channels financed by the Russian government, like *Sputnik* or RT, you soon begin to notice a pattern.

Naturally, all negative reports about the Russian government are missing, just like an Apple advertising brochure wouldn't mention details about working conditions in China. If something critical of Putin is mentioned, it's only in the context of an absurd attack by foreign media or politicians who apparently have no evidence. Apart from that, they're not principally concerned with spreading fake stories—that would be too obvious. What is presented is a daily selection from the thousands of breaking news items that support the broader picture, with tones and formulations that further the narrative: there's a huge difference in whether you speak of "rebels" or "terrorists," refer to someone as a "human rights activist" or an "agitator," or call a leader "legally elected" or "autocratic."
Reports that fit the government agenda are prominently placed, implying more relevance, even when they might be objectively not that important.

Media analysts have identified a number of these underlying narratives. They are, among others: the West wishes Russia only evil, and its media spreads anti-Russian propaganda. The Third World War is looming (this fits in with the previously mentioned headline). Europe is sinking into chaos. The U.S. is sinking into chaos. Putin is strong, as is Russia. And in general—don't believe anyone and don't trust any information.

The last point is by far the most deceitful, because it makes sense to any thinking person, but at the same time it implies that you can reach different conclusions for any incident. Thereby information from the *Guardian* or *New York Times* is put on the same level as information from RT, the conspiracy theories and gossip of Infowars.com, or any random post on Facebook. Welcome to the post-fact era, where news just becomes a matter of opinion.

A research report, published after two years of meticulous work, concludes that Malaysia Airlines flight MH17 was shot down over Ukrainian territory by a Russian Buk missile system? There must be a Western conspiracy against Russia behind it! And here are five other variations of how it could have happened: the plane wasn't shot down but just fell from the sky. The U.S. downed the plane to damage Russia's reputation. It was a Ukrainian ground-to-air missile. A Ukrainian fighter pilot attacked the plane in the air. Or there weren't any living beings on the plane in the first place—MH17 was loaded with dead bodies in Amsterdam and was flying on autopilot. All these theories can be found in Russian media.

When different versions of stories circulate, the natural reaction of the reader is to assume that the truth lies somewhere in the middle. This can be a trap, as sometimes there really is a true and a false version.

Many media outlets, not only in Russia, use narratives in their work, and some politicians do too. The narrative could also be: refugees are criminals. Or the *New York Times* is a propaganda outlet against Trump. Or Brexit opponents are financed by the EU. If there are enough true, half-true, and outright false pieces of information released that support these claims, the impression is reinforced that there must be some truth, even if occasionally some items of fake news are revealed as such. The narrative, however, should contain a "perceived truth" that seems plausible to many people. You won't get particularly far with "Hillary Clinton is an extraterrestrial from the planet Krikkit and plans to destroy Earth." The combination of a number of narratives has a stronger effect: for instance, "Donald Trump has achieved more than any other U.S. President" plus "the mainstream media is lying to us."

A B C
Laughing • СМЕЮЩИЙСЯ

An aspect of human behavior seen less frequently in Russia than in other countries—at least in public places. Someone who smiles at a stranger might be considered either crazy or a thief; a serious face, on the other hand, represents trustworthiness and commitment. In the digital world, the topic is tackled economically: the Russian close brackets smiley) consists of half as many symbols as the colon close brackets :) used in the rest of the world.

146   A survey in Germany revealed that the main reason for people's loss of trust in the established media was that information and stories you could read on Facebook and its ilk hadn't been picked up in the mainstream media.

A paradox: the greater the amount of information chaos, the more white noise of scandals and controversy, the more trust dwindles in those who have years of experience in sifting through information.

So, is the established media always right? Of course not; they provoke, simplify, and scandalize—the British tabloid *Sun* more, and the *Washington Post* less. And are they not also working to narratives to which the news is subordinated, just as the Russian media routinely claim? Yes, they are. A large majority of journalists in Western media would agree with the following two sentences and allow their essence to be incorporated in their work: democracy, as a system of governance, is relatively sensible. And pluralism, the acceptance of various opinions on a subject, is good for society.

Plus they believe in a "checks and balances" function of journalism: a critical view on government decisions is a crucial part of the job.

And precisely here lies the difference from RT and *Sputnik*. You won't find any critical words about Vladimir Putin or investigative reports on technological flaws of the Black Sea Fleet. And you won't find a large plurality of opinions. Who needs "fake news" when the selection of news items, their tone, and their headlines are enough to paint the picture you want?

It is, however, even more effective if you also manage to spread a few made-up stories. It's never been easier than it is today to reach a large audience. Particularly sensational news, regardless of whether it's true or false, reaches many people on Facebook. During my travels in Russia the story was going around in the U.S. that Pope Francis, in a historic move, had recommended that all American Catholics vote for the presidential candidate Trump. The fake report from WTOE 5 News

147

(the Russians are not behind it) got almost 900,000 shares on Facebook; a report by Snopes.com saying that it was absolute nonsense, only 67,000.

The USSR had a long tradition of inventing stories. One active measure of anti-American propaganda, for instance, was the story that HIV spread from a bioweapon operation initiated by the U.S. To this day many people consider it plausible, although the relevant secret documents of the KGB have long been released and no evidence exists.

A case from 2014 also shows that not all Russian fairy tales are about Baba Yaga. *Channel One*, the most popular TV broadcaster in the country, reported on Ukrainian nationalists who had nailed a three-year-old boy to a billboard right in the middle of the city of Sloviansk. A weeping sole witness named Galina Pyshniak gave her account in front of rolling cameras.

A reporter from the independent newspaper *Novaya Gazeta* visited the alleged scene and interviewed the locals. No one could confirm the incident, which would have caused uproar in the city. Also, a number of details in Pyshniak's testimony were false, including the name and size of the central square. But the original account reached a larger public than the later doubts.

Who makes the effort to check sources for every Facebook post? Or thinks about who is financing the source, about which self-interests the authors might be propagating?

In Volgograd, when I spent some time with David, the backpacker from New Zealand, he told me he was a big fan of RT because he could get information there that was withheld elsewhere. When I told him that RT was one hundred percent financed by the Kremlin, he didn't believe me at first. But he did firmly believe that soy sauce was causing a worrying feminization of the world because it contains estrogenlike substances.

I've done a bit of research and can reassure you that according to rigorous scientific studies, no harm has so far been detected from soy sauce consumption.

Internalizing the don't-trust-any-information mantra leads shrewd people to be even more persistent about searching for sources and to make use of their power of judgment, honed over years of making assessments.

Less astute or lazier people make things easy for the populists. With so much uncertainty, isn't it far easier when some charismatic guy has already sifted out what's true and false? How comforting to only have to believe this one opinion maker, who can sort all new pieces of information into a frame that he's created. How much more satisfying it is to hold the certainty that soy sauce feminizes men (no more Chinese food for me, then) than to express the less sensational position: "There's a high probability that it doesn't, but we can't definitively prove the opposite."

I look up from my mobile phone and out of the train window.

Truth No. 11:
In Siberia there are a hell of a lot of birch trees; that can be said with certainty.

MY OWN DACHA

YEVGENI, DRESSED ONLY in orange boxer shorts, greets me on the eighth floor of a high-rise in the new housing development area of Krasnoobsk. "Sorry, I'm just working out at the moment," says the IT engineer. He puts on his cycling gloves and does ten pull-ups on a bar fitted to the door frame with no visible sign of effort. He has short, spiky hair, a healthy-looking tan unusual for those in his profession, and eyes sparkling with enthusiasm.

"Do you eat everything?" he asks on returning to the kitchen. Yes, I do. "Good." Everything looks new and clean in the apartment. He puts some eggs into a pan and sits at the table to slice tomatoes, placing a cucumber in front of me to chop. "Unfortunately, there's been a change of plan," he says. "I wasn't expecting it, but I have to go to work tomorrow at six AM and I'm out of Novosibirsk until late in the evening."

"Okay, shall I get up with you and spend the day in the city?"

"No, you can stay in my dacha, then you're independent. Mayonnaise or sour cream with your salad?"

He goes back into the hall and with brisk, practiced movements does another twelve pull-ups. Then we eat and talk about traveling in Russia. Last year he went hiking with two visitors from Latvia and one from Germany on Olkhon Island in Lake Baikal. "It was fantastic. Actually, there are too many Chinese on the island, but they don't go hiking with their rolling suitcases." I make a mental note to add Olkhon to my itinerary. "But one thing was funny: the parents of the German girl were panic-stricken when she told them she was planning to visit Russia. People have real funny notions because they only know Russia from TV."

"Some Russians have funny notions about Europe because they only know it from TV," I reply.

"Now, be honest, if you had the choice who would you want to conquer Europe—Russians or radical Muslims?"

"I would prefer not to be conquered at all."

"In Russia a wide range of people and cultures live together, respecting each other. There's no reason to be afraid of such a country."

"How advanced are the plans for conquering Europe?"

"Forget it! It was just a thought. Have you got a headlamp?"

We carry my luggage to two bikes in front of the house and pedal off. After a few minutes on the asphalt roads of the residential area we enter a birch forest. The path is not particularly good and we have to ride slowly because of the roots and uneven ground. It smells of fresh herbs and the ground crackles from the fallen foliage.

I have only known Yevgeni for about an hour and we're riding off into the darkness through a wilderness which is only visible ten yards ahead in the lamplight. Maybe this would be a good time to become a bit mistrustful. My gut instinct after

151

eleven years of couchsurfing training says: *No need to worry.* The only challenge will be finding my way back in daylight, as we've made quite a number of turns.

After about ten minutes we reach a metal gate with the words *Tichie Sori*—"peaceful sunrise"—above it. We pull up at house number eighty-six on lane number six. A yapping gray-white terrier circles me.

"That's Knoppa, she loves people with backpacks because she thinks we're about to set off on a journey," says Yevgeni.

In the darkness I can make out a house and a garden with tomatoes and cucumbers. This is not the place for arachnophobes; there are two fat spiders just above the entrance. There is a kitchenette, a bedroom, unconventionally laid electricity cables, and an attic that can only be reached by a homemade ladder from outside—"That's where I prefer sleeping." After a little tour of the house, Yevgeni departs, saying "Make yourself at home" before pedaling off into the night. I now have my own dacha. With a dog.

After many weeks of sharing other people's living space, my own realm suits me fine. Couchsurfing is not a relaxing way of spending vacations, regardless of how nice the hosts are. You always have to adjust to someone else's plans, to be thankful for everything, to comply with their wishes. When you arrive at the tenth or fifteenth host, it's less exciting than it was at the beginning; the getting-acquainted small talk starts to feel like an imitation of previous introductions and the fifth uncomfortable bed causes more backaches than the first. By the same token, it would be highly unfair to take out my occasional travel fatigue on those who aren't to blame for it and who do me a huge favor by inviting me.

I'm often asked what the hosts get out of it. Yevgeni wrote in his profile that he wanted to give something back after being so well looked after on his own travels. Murad, in Grozny, told me that foreign visitors are like a breath of fresh air as the daily grind brings only frustration, and on top of that he has been able to improve his English enormously thanks to the practice. I have had more than a hundred guests and even when working a forty-hour week, have always been happy to feel like I'm in travel mode when people tell me about their adventures. On top of this, I visit places in Hamburg with guests that alone I never would have explored, and have come to appreciate my own city all the more. Some friendships are ongoing; sometimes we arrange return visits. Sometimes a guest is a mismatch, always going on about how he is only interested in saving money and behaving as if he were in a hotel. But with time you develop an instinct about who is likely to be a pleasant guest, using hints either from their initial email or from reading their profile.

153

The next day I just stay in my little summerhouse and watch green, yellow, and red tomatoes grow. I do nothing other than sit around, stroke Knoppa, and enjoy the view from my favorite place, at the entrance to the attic on the top of the homemade ladder.

In the garden diagonally opposite, an elderly lady in a kind of leopard-patterned negligee, blue rubber gloves, and a hairnet rakes away at a flowerbed. A couple of houses away, someone is listening to Russian electro-pop songs. Knoppa snoozes in the grass, crickets chirp, birds twitter; on the horizon there is smoke from the chimneys of a power station. Russian country life, just outside the city limits. The houses of the dacha settlement have pointed gables and spacious attics. The sun is scorching and it's already ninety degrees at midday. You need no down jacket in Siberia if you visit in summer.

Only two more things happen this day: two dragonflies mate and I get a WhatsApp message from Yevgeni: "Please open the door to the greenhouse to let some heat out," an instruction I'm happy to follow.

CHEVY OR ZHIGULI?

NADYA LIKES MOTORBIKES, fast cars, and sleek yachts and knows all the barkeepers in Novosibirsk. Her voice is as cool and cutting as Siberian ice on a January night; she can switch expressions from a deadly serious sulk to a radiant smile and back in a fraction of a second. Like two people in one body. Her divorce came through a few days ago after a year of marriage to an Armenian businessman, which was spent living in a luxury villa on the island of Phuket in Thailand. When she got home she did what many do in such life-changing situations and went straight to her hairstylist.

She sits opposite me in a Caucasian restaurant with a meticulous pageboy haircut, brown eyes, and a blue summer dress. We eat lamb soup and chicken kebab, drink Russian pale ale, and talk of life, travel, and music. We soon discover that as teenagers we were both fans of Queen. I rule as completely ridiculous her submission that *The Miracle* was their best album and counter with *A Night at the Opera* and *Queen II*. Still, at least we can agree on *A Day at the Races* being an absolute classic.

Does she know the Altai region south of Novosibirsk, my next destination? Of course, she has been there. "It was a disaster because of the tour guide. Everybody wanted to do something different; we fought the whole time. One scandal after the other." I quickly notice that "scandal" is one of her favorite words, having roughly the same meaning in Russian, English, and German.

We wander through the city for a bit. In front of the theater (next premiere: Kafka's *The Trial*) a band is playing; the singer is trying to sound like Jim Morrison, flaunting his masculinity with some wobbly English. In Lenin Square a muscular fire-eater is performing as his topless assistant swirls a skull-and-crossbones flag. Around them there are grim-looking men with bikes and leather jackets with the logo of the Night Wolves, an infamous motorcycle gang. A busker nearby with a Western guitar sings "Sweet Dreams (Are Made of This)." There's a full moon; the wolves on the jackets seem to howl at it. Quite a lot going on in Novosibirsk on a Friday night.

Back in my private dacha I ask Nadya via WhatsApp whether she feels like accompanying me on a weeklong tour of the Altai region.

Her response is a picture message with a screenshot of a car rental website showing a bright-yellow Chevrolet Camaro sports car. I was actually thinking more along the lines of a Zhiguli, a Russian version of the old East German Trabi or the Indian Ambassador. We meet in the middle and go for a vw Polo, then begin to argue over the best route.

Originally I wasn't planning on renting a car, which is why even though I had packed my international driver's license, I had failed to inspect it closely. When I do inspect it more closely, the expiry date doesn't make me happy at all.

DRIVING,
RUSSIAN-STYLE

"**WE'VE GOT A** slight problem," explains Nadya to the clerk in the office of the car rental company Eurazcar. The keys are already on the glass table in front of us. A picture of a Formula 1 racing car hangs on one wall; on the other, a map; on an Ikea shelf next to it, an icon. Faith, speed, Russia: the triptych of the ultimate road adventure.

"What kind of problem?"

"The European driving license is valid, but the international one has expired."

"Have you got a certified translation of the European license?"

"No."

"When did it expire?"

"February first."

"That's only a couple of months ago."

"February first, 2008."

"Oh." He smiles bleakly, as only Russians can do.

"But I'm a web designer and a Photoshop pro. We can take a photo of the license and simply change the expiry date," Nadya suggests. "If you show a photo instead of the original there is just a 500 ruble fine, I've checked on Google."

"Hmm."

In a great many countries on this planet a car rental clerk would tell a client to go to hell after such a proposition. At Eurazcar in Novosibirsk the man, cool as a cucumber, copies both the international and the European license numbers into the contract and gives us the keys.

"How did you manage to get us out of that?" I ask Nadya in the corridor.

"Mutual interest," she explains. "We want to travel, he wants our money. There is no reason for him not to give us the car." His main concern was that we stick to the speed limits. It's Sunday and there are extra traffic cops on the streets hoping for more business than usual. Speeding raps get the rental company in trouble.

The black car doesn't look like what we would consider a Polo—it's a notchback sedan with automatic gears only produced and sold in Russia.

Nadya names it "Polya." You have to establish this before setting off, she says. *Polya* is the short form of *Polina* and sounds somewhat Russian; if our car isn't going to be a Lada, Zhiguli, or a UAZ, at least it has a Russian name. However, if Polya had known what was in store for her, she probably would have immediately driven up the stairs to the fifth floor of the office block and pleaded with the rental clerk not to accept Photoshopped driving licenses.

Nadya says "*S Bogom*"—"with God," then we drive to her parents' house, where she loads up the car with a huge backpack, a weighty metal cooking pot, a large suitcase, rain boots with a Mickey Mouse print, and two smaller backpacks. "We're traveling for a week, not a year," I remind her.

"I'm a woman," she reminds me. "Can you change tires?"

"With Google, for sure," I reply.

"Me neither," she says. And then we head south.

On the outskirts of town we make our first stop, at a shopping mall called GiGant. Nadya loads up the cart with canned fish, potatoes, and "CCCP" condensed milk ("the best in the world"); we also find an angular camping gas cooker, and then we're ready for the highway.

According to Maps.me it's five hours to Gorno-Altaysk, our first stop for the night. "If I drive, four hours," Nadya promises, and gets behind the wheel. What follows is a lesson in driving, Russian-style. The cultural differences I observe are best illustrated by a short quiz:

159

Passing is a safe option when...

a) there is a distance of at least 150 feet from oncoming traffic after completing the maneuver.

b) you assume that the oncoming driver is forward-thinking

enough to slam on his brakes at the last moment to avoid a head-on collision.

A red triangle with an exclamation mark...
a) is a warning of an approaching hazard.
b) could mean anything. As the worst axle-breaking potholes are not usually marked, it's not worth braking when you spot such a sign.

While driving at night with your headlights on high beam, when oncoming traffic approaches, you should...
A) dip them.
b) be thankful that you have better visibility because this means you can drive more safely than the other driver.

If a cow or other animal big enough to damage the front of the car on collision is on the road, the best response is...
a) to stop.
b) to honk your horn.

An important part of a successful passing maneuver consists of...
a) performing it in clear visibility while driving proactively.
b) screaming: "*Davay davay! Blin! Davay davay* DAVAY!"

On a dirt road, when an oncoming vehicle stirs up so much dust that visibility is severely impeded, you should...
160   a) brake and wait until the car has passed and the dust cloud has dispersed.
b) put your foot on the gas so the dust cloud is behind you as quickly as possible.

You can recognize a car wash by...
a) an entrance with large, brightly colored rotating brushes.
b) a sexist poster of barely clad ladies spraying a sports car.

A math problem: A road has two lanes, one going in each direction; each lane is 7.5 feet wide, giving a total width of 15 feet. What is the maximum number of 6-foot-wide cars that can fit on the road?
a) two.
b) three (the gravel shoulder is not just there for decoration).

Abandoning a passing maneuver by braking and merging back to your previous position...
a) can avoid accidents in emergencies.
b) should be practiced as often as possible so that you get better at it.

The scoring is simple. If the majority of your answers are b), then you are Russian. If the majority of your answers are a), you are not Russian.

THERE IS NO doubt about Nadya's nationality. "*Davay davay davay! Blin!*" she shouts repeatedly. Even with her foot flat on the gas pedal she doesn't seem pleased with Polya's acceleration. *Blin* means "pancake," but is also a universally deployable (and pretty cute) expletive. I imagine if more people in the world knew that Russians shout "pancake!" when something gets on their nerves, they wouldn't find this country half as threatening as they do. *Davay* is a magic word because it suits almost any situation. It can mean "come on" but also "gimme," "bye," "take care," or "let's go." Thanks to its versatility it's possible to conduct small talk with just this word (in a small gathering of sober Russians for three minutes, with drunk Russians up to half an hour) without anybody noticing you don't speak their language.

After four and a half hours we reach Gorno-Altaysk in darkness. With a population of 56,000, it's the largest city in the autonomous Republic of Altai. Nadya informs me of the local peculiarities: "We have to be careful in this region; the people who live here are a bit different. Poor, without internet—they'll steal the car with everything in it while we're off hiking." Tonight we're not going hiking, but have a hotel with an illuminated parking lot. So it seems we're safe for now.

SUNSET AND *BANYA*

THE M52 RUNS right through the middle of the Altai Republic over a number of passes from Gorno-Altaysk to the border of Mongolia. There are a few dirt roads branching off from the main road, but a large portion of the region is difficult to access because of the rivers, mountains, and the many thousands of lakes. Mount Belukha, in the southwest, with a height of 14,783 feet, is the highest mountain in Siberia.

Many houses have hexagonal *ails*, traditional wooden buildings in the garden that resemble yurts. At the Sema Pass, souvenir dealers with weather beaten faces sell Mongolian camel's wool socks, Altai honey, and herbal teas that look as if someone has just walked out into the steppes and tried to gather grasses with as many different colors as possible. A sign with a blue arrow indicates that it is 1,950 miles to Moscow, 1,650 miles to Beijing, and 2,950 miles to Berlin. A golden eagle circles in the sky above.

Accompanying us beside the road is the Katun River, a fairly wild and powerful representative of its kind, with cyan waters and whitecaps. Birch trees, aspen, and larches decorate the woodland slopes. Soon the first three- and four-thousanders loom to the right, magnificent snowy peaks beyond the yellow steppes. "The air is clear and I can do as I wish here"—so says a tea dealer in camouflage clothing about the merits of his homeland.

We take turns driving. As Nadya needs twenty percent less and I need twenty percent more time than calculated by our navigation device, it's easy to figure out how long it will take to get to the next village. The asphalt is mostly okay, but you always have to be on the lookout for potholes or stones on the road. "Russia has two problems: bad roads and stupid people," says Nadya. I tell her that in my travels so far I haven't met any really stupid Russians. Up to now I've been spared the notorious *gopniks*—young small-time mobsters of the suburbs. "Spend two days in Novosibirsk with me and all that will change," Nadya promises.

What does she like about Russia? "The expanse, the size, nature." The Altai Republic has all that in abundance. The M52 is one of the most spectacular roads in the country. The fauna in the surroundings adds to its reputation; toward the Mongolian border, yaks and wild camels wander across the road. Kosh-Agach, our southernmost destination, is a disappointment. With less than six inches of annual rainfall, it's the driest inhabited place in Russia. It seems like a neglected outpost in no-man's-land: dusty, with garbage in the roadside ditches. However, the decrepit wooden huts with corrugated iron roofs in turquoise, green, and red seem to have been freshly painted. An earthquake caused much damage here in 2003. As if the people didn't have enough problems already, with winter temperatures of minus fifty-eight degrees Fahrenheit and summer plagues of insects whose bites can trigger encephalitis. At the roadside I discover a curious hand-painted sign with *Beware! Ticks* written on it.

The most modern building is a monitoring facility of the FSB, which has signal receivers pointing toward Mongolia. The translated name of the village is "the last tree," but that's a bit of an exaggeration, as far and wide there is not a single tree to be seen.

Our only interactions with the locals are with a grumpy café owner serving watery instant coffee and sweet cookies, and a drunk on the street begging for money.

Nadya doesn't feel at ease here and can't understand why, despite the evident lack of charm in Kosh-Agach, I still want to snap a few photos. She couldn't know that I have a secret soft spot for desolate places. Eventually I tear myself away; we drive back along the same street and start looking for accommodation, as it's already late afternoon.

"I want to see the sunset," says Nadya. "And I want a beer. And a *banya*." She reaches for her cell phone, which is connected to the car radio, and with her right hand scrolls through her playlist for some suitable music, her left hand still on the steering wheel.

She suggests "I Want It All" by Queen.

I suggest that she keep her eyes on the road and not on her cell phone.

Unfortunately, the evening sun is not particularly well placed. For a good view we have to weave around Aktru, Maashey-Bash, and Kurkurek, three mountains all roughly thirteen thousand feet high. To the left a neat collection of wooden cabins appears. A *Mesta yest* sign means there are rooms available. "Let's stop here and tomorrow we will have a stunning sunrise," I suggest. To the east the valley opens out to the glorious wide steppes, framed by snow-capped peaks.

"I want to see the sun *set*," says Nadya, and she steps on the gas.

"Where do you want to go?" I inquire. On the outward journey we had already noted that there weren't many chances of finding accommodation on this stretch of the road.

"I saw a house with a *banya* in Inya," she says.

"Inya is ninety miles away and it will be dark in forty-five minutes."

"Then just to the next valley. The sunset of the century awaits us there. Hang tight!" The sky is already turning red; she accelerates just a bit more.

"*Blin*! Does the road have to get worse right here?" The road becomes bumpier, the tires flicking up small stones. A 40 speed limit sign induces Nadya to slow down to 85. A tiny Jesus figure dangles beneath the rearview mirror. The way he's been jolted about today, it's a miracle he hasn't thrown up.

All that racing didn't help one bit; the sun sinks behind the mountains.

"Shit!" says Nadya.

Twenty minutes later we reach the next *Mesta yest* wooden cabins. They seem to be brand new and comfortable, but unfortunately they're all occupied.

An elderly man with a military cap approaches us and says that he has some equally attractive accommodation in the neighboring village of Aktash. Wooden cabins and a *banya* only five minutes from here. "And beer?" asks Nadya.

"In the supermarket, yes," he replies.

We accept. He calls his son, who then waits for us at the gas station. A dour character driving a UAZ Jeep. We buy some drinks, then follow him down an uneven dirt road full of potholes.

"Just the right terrain for his car," says Nadya sarcastically. Polya bobbles like a tiny boat in a heavy swell; rearview mirror Jesus hops up and down.

The accommodation touted as "equally attractive" proves to be an overgrown garden with a few warped forms that vaguely resemble wooden cabins. The dour son opens the door of one of them. "Fifteen hundred rubles a night, the *banya* is out of order," he says as his two customers' jaws drop all the way down. The first room is a cramped kitchen; beyond it is a bedroom with five single beds and an electric heater. The décor is colorful, but shows a glaring lack of sensitivity for shades that actually go together. It takes me a few seconds to grasp the concept, and then I get it. The mauve/red/green/pink/light-blue/yellow bedspreads, quilts, and carpets have been combined thematically rather than chromatically, following the principle that everything with flowers on it is fine.

The photos on the wall are also in violent breach of the "less is more" principle. A harsh naked bulb dangling from the ceiling illuminates cute kitten pictures, Japanese bird sketches, and a cocktail still life (a cocktail still life!). A forest and river motif has been framed by plastic ferns to accentuate the effect.

A B C

Masash and the Bear • МАША И МЕДВЕДЬ

A Russian animated TV series about a hedonistic young girl with ADHD and a kindhearted bear who, after years of working for a circus, now enjoys peace and quiet as a retiree. As expected from a pair of such varying backgrounds, their friendship is shaped by many conflicts of interest. Not only children enjoy the episodes. The most popular one has had over 2.4 billion views on YouTube, making it the most viewed cartoon in the world.

"We'll take it," I say.

"I'm not staying here a second," says Nadya.

"It'll take at least an hour before we find somewhere else."

"If I drive, forty minutes."

"Maybe we could get him to lower the price a bit?"

"Okay," she turns to the landlord. "Hey, my friend here is a bit stingy and thinks that it's too expensive, can we do something about that?"

The son calls his father and then offers us the room for 1,200 rubles. Nadya resigns herself to her fate. At least we got some beer—two bottles of *Barnaulskoye*.

"Did you call me 'a bit stingy'?" I ask.

"Well, I had to give him some reason or another for asking for a discount," answers the negotiating expert. She then crawls beneath her floral quilt with her cell phone and beer and says no more.

THE NEXT DAY, the only other cabin guests are having breakfast in a kind of wooden pavilion in the garden: a family with a fully laden small car who have been traveling in the region for a while. This is good news for us, as we're having a slight problem planning our route. We want to leave the highway soon, turning to the west to reach the mountain village of Tyungur. According to the map printed in the guidebook, there is no road there. Nadya's navigating system, however, shows a road some forty miles long and tells us that the trip will take two and a half hours. We ask the father of the breakfasting family. He consults his crumpled map and tells us that it seems perfectly possible. The alternative would involve a detour of more than a couple of hundred miles.

So we follow his advice and take the turn. At first it seems like a good decision; we are again following the Katun River, which snakes through the valley in a particularly attractive way.

Truth No. 12:
Nature has a better sense of aesthetics than people.

Today Nadya is wearing a pink T-shirt with "I love evil" printed on it. She gives me a mogul slope driving lesson: "If you drive fast on a bad road it's better for the car," she says. "Then you just fly over all the holes and you don't feel so sick." Sound advice, but it still leaves quite a bit of scope for interpretation as far as ideal speed is concerned.

The local sheep, horses, and cows all look remarkably healthy, but are also remarkably assertive about who owns the dirt road. The enchanting bobak marmots have better survival instincts and hurry to get out of the way.

A large puddle, unfortunately, can't be scared away. We stop to look at it more closely. Now Nadya's Mickey Mouse rain boots prove their worth. She sinks so deep into the puddle that she only just avoids the water flowing into her boots. "You wanted adventure—well, here it is," she says, then gets back into the car and drives with gusto through the obstacle. In a village, I suggest asking someone about the state of the road ahead. Nadya prefers to press on. The navi device continues to stubbornly insist that we're on the right route; common sense soon suggests the opposite. The surface is no longer just bumpy—it goes up and down steeply. We get out and walk on a few hundred yards to better judge the conditions. The route goes down steeply for a while—pretty uncomfortably, with large boulders—but further down, alongside the river, it looks somewhat better. In an emergency we would have to wait a long time for assistance; we're already twenty miles off the highway and there's no cell phone reception.

"Let's try it," I say.

"Let's turn back," says Nadya.

"You're the one who wanted adventure," I say.

"Will you call the rental company to tell them that we've trashed the car?" she asks.

Okay, we turn back.

About halfway home we come across another car. Locals in a four-wheel-drive Toyota. They just laugh when asked if it's possible to drive to Tyungur.

"With *that* car? Are you completely crazy?"

The family from earlier this morning are sitting in the next car we encounter. "We'll take a look for ourselves," they say as we try to dissuade them from going on. Stubbornness, thy name is Russia. But still, they have four-wheel drive. "There's a Russian saying," says Nadya as we drive on. "The bigger the car, the farther the tractor has to go." In other words: if a road is leading to disaster anyway, then at least in a small car it happens quicker.

The family consists of two parents, an aunt, a daughter of twenty years old at most, and a grandchild. "Why do Russian women have children so young?" I ask Nadya.

"Women's bodies are healthier then and that's better for the children," she replies. "On top of that, when you have a child at eighteen, most of the rough stuff is behind you by the time you're twenty-three and then you can study or get on with your career."

"But the men often seem to disappear. In no other country have I seen so many young single moms."

"It's better to get a divorce with kids than without them. The men have to pay 25 percent of their monthly salary for child support. Also you don't fall into such a deep hole as you have something that gives life a purpose. After marrying, many women try to get pregnant as soon as possible."

Nevertheless, there are few countries with higher abortion rates than Russia. Statistically, every woman here has at least one abortion in her lifetime. This has a long tradition: Russia allowed the procedure as early as 1920, becoming the first country to do so. Nowadays, as the population is declining, the Orthodox Church actively campaigns for large families and President Putin introduced a fat bonus of 429,409 rubles (US$7,400) for every woman having a second child.

But back to the dirt road. Now we suddenly have to cover three hundred extra miles to reach our couchsurfing destination for tonight. And that's not our only problem. In Ust-Koksa and its surroundings, a foreigner needs to have registration, which must be applied for weeks in advance—a formality I hadn't bothered with. As I talk about this with Nadya I imagine our conversation would make a good skit demonstrating the difference between clichéd German and clichéd Russian responses.

GERMANY: "Let's have a plan in case we're stopped."

RUSSIA: "If you worry about it too much it's bound to go wrong."

GERMANY: "I'd be less worried if we had a plan."

RUSSIA: "Hey, it'll be okay."

GERMANY: "We'll say we were just traveling past and took the wrong turn, okay?"

RUSSIA: "I want an ice cream."

GERMANY: "Ice cream? Here? We haven't passed a single café for hours."

RUSSIA: "An ice cream. Chocolate."

(Not ten minutes later, in the next village, a small roadside kiosk materializes with a fully packed freezer.)

"Told you!" says Russia.

A PLACE WITH
GOOD KARMA

I'M A CITY person and have never stayed with anybody who had a real well in the garden. It has a long, bowed wooden pole for a lever and a bucket hanging from it—a technique thousands of years old. About twenty-five feet below, the water from a very special river collects. "The Katun is thought to have stronger healing properties than the Ganges," says Irina, our host in Ust-Koksa. "People who bathe in it feel something." Beside the house are a barn filled with what look like prehistoric implements and a small outhouse with a pit toilet.

"My landlord is an eighty-seven-year-old Old Believer. I pay just two thousand rubles a month," she says. Two thousand rubles is around thirty-three U.S. dollars. Old Believers are followers of the opponents to the ecclesiastical reforms instigated by Patriarch Nikon in the mid-seventeenth century. A group of them founded Ust-Koksa in 1807 after they had to flee from the established church to the mountains. To this day in Siberia there are a number of remote Old Believer villages without electricity or running water. I would have dearly loved to stay with one of them, but this minority group is not particularly well represented on the internet, so I'll have to make do with the second-best alternative—the tenant of an Old Believer's house.

"You're my first guests," says Irina as she prepares a self-picked herbal tea. The staunch vegetarian is thirty, has a rosy complexion, and is dressed like a hippie, in vividly colored clothing. She came to Altai a year ago from Saint Petersburg because she wanted to escape the big city, and now she works as an artist. She specializes in round wooden plaques decorated with old Russian ornaments and painted flower-tendril creations with stuck-on colored stones. Apart from these she is particularly interested in Maya calendars, chakras, power places, and the TV singing competition show *The Voice*.

And herbal remedies. They are the most important economic industry in Ust-Koksa, at least until the small airport reopens and brings in more mountaineering tourists. For two months a year, many locals tramp off into the wilds searching for rhodiola, or roseroot. Here it is known as golden root and is thought to help ease stress and depression. Recently a study of U.S. scientists stated that its active ingredients increased the life span of fruit flies by 24 percent. It's hardly surprising, then, that the plant is a bestseller beyond Siberia. Red root, a member of the sweetvetch family, is similarly sought after and is said to be good for the nervous system and libido. However, the red root plant needs to grow for thirty years before it can be used as a herbal remedy. Its stocks are so limited that it appears on the Red List of Threatened Species and cannot be legally picked in the wild. For a small stake in the profits, however, local officials will often turn a blind eye, and the pharmaceutical company buyers won't ask any awkward questions. "Many people earn 100,000 rubles"—about US$1,600—"in a couple of weeks from picking roots," says Irina. "They then don't have to work for the rest of the year."

Rents and the cost of living are low in Altai. You can buy a house for less than 500,000 rubles, one like Irina's—without a bath or sewage pipes but at least with electricity. One of her friends even has a proper shower: "Every now and then I invite myself over to her place for a shower," Irina says. I can only dream of such house prices in Hamburg. If the Siberian winters weren't so extreme, I would seriously consider moving here.

One of Russia's most famous landscape painters, Nikolai Roerich, had the same idea ninety years ago. Besides painting, he excelled as a philosopher, author, and politician and had a spectacular white beard. His house was in the neighboring village of Verkh-Uymon, which today houses a museum featuring his work. "That is a place with good karma," promises Irina.

Roerich saw a great future for the region. "Who has said that Altai is cruel and unapproachable? Whose heart has become fearful of the austere power and beauty?"[7] is quoted on one of the displays.

The paintings in the exhibit try to capture the spiritual aspects of a mountain excursion, with exaggerated colorfulness. Many depict the mountains of the Himalayas in India and Nepal, but the local Belukha Mountain also serves as a motif. The museum guide tells us of the mysterious happenings surrounding the creation of one painting. "Actually, it's a two-day trip to that spot at the foot of the mountain. Roerich, however, only made day trips when painting. Maybe the spirits helped him."

You often hear stories of supernatural beings here. "Belukha is said to be the gateway to the mystical paradise Shambhala, also known as Shangri-la," says Irina, full of respect. She is planning a hiking tour to Akkem Lake, near the four-thousander. "But first I have to find my inner peace. You should only go there once your body and spirit are in harmony."

Originally Nadya and I wanted to make a tour to Akkem Lake, but Irina warns me about staying too long without a permit. "It's border country and if they catch you the officials don't have a sense of humor." I decide to return another time. When body and law are in harmony.

CAR KAPUT

INSTEAD OF HEADING to the idyllic lake we set off in the other direction, to Chemal in the north. Friends of Nadya have booked a two-day horse riding tour there and invited us along. We bump along a dusty dirt road through the steppes with round rolls of hay and indifferent cows. People here joke that if you drive along the roads here with a bag of milk in the trunk, after half an hour you'll have cream, and I now know what they mean.

"Will you visit me in prison, if I happen to get caught without a permit?" I ask as we pass a sign reading *Border Control*.

"Every day," says Nadya.

We're in luck: the post is deserted; it's already dark. After a good three hours on the mogul-road we rejoin the highway. Baby-bum-smooth asphalt from now on; we glide instead of driving. It's a car commercial come to life. And, of course, Nadya really steps on the gas.

We both see the sharp-edged, fist-sized stone too late. Polya jolts right over it. There's swearing in Russian, German, and English, jamming of brakes, and we stop on the gravel shoulder.

We take stock: It's just before 11:00 PM. The right front tire looks bad—it's pretty flat. The back tire sounds bad—it's leaking air. Fifteen minutes later, it's breathed its last breath. The ratio of available spare tires to the number of flat ones is 1:2.

In such situations, it's extremely unwelcome to read "No Network" on your cell phone display. We look on Nadya's navi for the nearest roadside assistance services. It answers that help is at hand sixteen hundred miles away, in Ulyanovsk, on the Volga; the trip will take forty-two hours. I've lost confidence in the thing after it tried to send us to our doom in the mountains, so I suggest a little walk in the hope of gaining access to the internet from a higher point.

Next to the road somewhere, we hear the splashing of water; because of the lack of light pollution, the night sky is so grandiose that it's almost an affront. "We've got enough gas to leave the car running all night for the heater," says Nadya.

"We've got half a roll of salami to eat," I add. Today we are a man/woman skit: she wants warmth, he wants food.

Five hundred yards further on I actually have one bar of reception. Et voilà: according to Maps.me it is only eighty-odd miles to the nearest towing services, in Gorno-Altaysk. That sounds better. Nadya calls to order a tow truck. We climb back into the car, put on warm clothes, eat salami, and listen to Queen at nightclub volume. Every five minutes the headlights of cars and trucks breeze by.

And sometime an eternity later, a pair of headlights slow down and a UAZ Ranger recovery vehicle pulls up next to us. Two men in dark track pants and light-colored sneakers get out and introduce themselves as Danil and Ararat. "From Germany? You're not used to such roads, eh?" Danil says, and laughs. He looks to be in his mid-forties and his assistant seems about half his age. From their erratic movements as they apply the crowbar to the wheel rims, I realize that Nadya's call must have reached them in the middle of a pleasant bout of drinking.

"Are you man and wife? Aren't Russian men good enough?" Danil asks Nadya. There's a distinctive smell of alcohol on his breath.

Soon a massive crane slowly hoists up our poor Polya. It sways back and forth so violently that we have to grab the bumpers to stop it from colliding with the truck's windows. Then we sit four in a row in the driver's cabin, although there's only space for three. Danil calls his wife. "Sorry, I'm going to be late. Please don't lock the door. We've got a German with a kaput car." He says it as if it's the craziest thing in the world.

The crane's hook swings around in front of the windshield; Arabic belly-dancing music blares out of Ararat's cell phone. Suddenly the road surface is strewn with millions of moths, which continues for several miles; it's like a scene from a horror movie. They make absolutely no effort to escape from oncoming traffic. "Because of them we had two springs this year," says Danil. "They completely wiped out the first leaves, then everything had to grow again."

He stops at a gas station and forgets to pull the hand brake. As he opens the gas cap, the vehicle begins to roll slowly, directly toward a kiosk. With a scream, he runs to the door, jumps in—banging his head in the process—and grabs the brake. Raucous laughter. "That wouldn't happen in Germany, eh?" he says.

179

After about a hundred-mile drive we pull up at a small roadside workshop. On the sign outside: *Shinomontazh*—tire "montage," or mounting. Words borrowed from French have a special *scharm* in Russia: before a *massazh* you can dab on some *Letual odekolon* (L'étoile eau de cologne) that you packed in your *bagazh*.

Less charming is what Danil is now doing to our car. He is hammering away at one of the wheel rims, as if he had to first kill it before reusing it. A bit of *odekolon* would do the garage no harm, as it stinks of glue and paint. We are seated on two threadbare armchairs right next to the place where freshly sprayed cars are brought to dry. Danil brings us two pinecones as our evening meal. A genuine gourmet snack can be found beneath the scales: the pine nuts of the Siberian pine.

Eventually it turns out to be a good night. Danil manages to whip the wheels into shape, Ararat gazes off into space, and Nadya and I nibble away at the nuts. Shortly after 3:00 AM, Polya is up and running again and we can move on. However, with the spare tires, we have a speed cap of maximum fifty miles per hour.

An hour later Danil calls up to ask if all is well. Good guy. Or does he know something about the repairs that we don't? It doesn't matter; those two guys burned the midnight oil for us instead of putting us off until the next day, and you have to appreciate that. Shortly before sunrise we reach Chemal.

Truth No. 13:
Russia's service sector is better than its reputation.

When 105 horsepower causes so many problems, maybe you should downsize to one. The next morning, after visiting the local *Shinomontazh* (one of the tires was flat again), we drive the forty miles to Edigan, a village with two hundred inhabitants. There was a slight misunderstanding at the planning stage, which is why we're half an hour late. "Be on the lookout for a white Range Rover and a couple of very angry people sitting on horses," Nadya instructs me as we near the meeting point.

I soon spot the Range Rover, but not the angry people. Alexander and Galina enthusiastically greet Nadya; they haven't seen each other for years. The rest of the group consists of Juliya, nine, Galina's daughter; Yevgeni and Natalya, a couple both over fifty; and Alexey, a twenty-six-year-old IT expert and keen hunter. Our guide is Nikita, who is eighteen. The top half of him, with his baseball cap, sunglasses, and hoodie, looks like Eminem; the bottom half, thanks to his thigh-high waders, like a fly-fisherman. We lash waterproof bags to the saddles and set off.

In general, handling horses is not that complex. *Brrr* means "whoa," *noo* means "get going," digging your heels into the flanks means "giddyap," and you use the reins to steer. At least that's what Nikita shows the beginners. Pros can control the direction by shifting their weight.

In the run-up to the trip I imagined us like Genghis Khan and the Golden Horde galloping across the steppes. But initially it's more like Cowboy Eminem and the Six Sacks of Flour. Beneath us, seven pointedly indifferent horses trot along a forest path in single file.

My horse is called Chalka and stops being indifferent far quicker than I would have wished. Piqued by an attempt at passing by one of his kind, the stallion lapses into something that to an onlooker probably seems like a pleasant trot but for me feels like galloping headlong into battle. After a mile (my perception) or rather forty yards (the perception of an objective observer; and no, here the truth doesn't lie somewhere in

the middle), my steed begins to calm down. Only in the coming hours do Chalka and I slowly become friends.

A B C
National Anthem · ГОСУДАРСТВЕННЫЙ ГИМН

One of the first changes instigated by Vladimir Putin after
his inauguration in 2000 was reinstating the Soviet Union
national anthem. Or at least the tune, which is actually
pretty good. The text, however, had to be reworked. Lines
like: "In the victory of Communism's immortal ideal / We
see the future of our land"[8] were no longer deemed to be
contemporary, and became: "Wide expanses for dreams
and living / Are opened for us by the coming years."[9]

In the evening we pitch our tents in a clearing and make
a campfire. A little bit further up a slope the view is sensational: rows of hill silhouettes in shades of gray vanish into the
distance in the evening mists like a theater backdrop. Nikita
chops up wood with a huge ax and tells us a bit about his life.
He started riding twelve years ago because there wasn't much
else interesting going on in his village. In summer there are
groups of tourists and in winter, hunters. They have to apply
for permits in advance for the numbers of stags, deer, or birds
that they're allowed to shoot. "But often they drink so much
that they can't ride, let alone shoot," he says with a hoarse
laugh. Nadya advises me to study him carefully. "You'd have
difficulty finding a more perfect example of a young rural Russian," she says. "A bit overconfident, a bit too cool, and always

with a curse on his lips. But practical, not a slacker, gallant toward women, and kind to kids."

For the evening meal there is *Dushonka* canned meat, slightly smoked pork with rice, and *kognak*. And raw bits of onion. Galina is convinced they're the best food for campers: "You are guaranteed not to become ill on the trip." Empty cans are simply thrown onto the fire. The seemingly endless availability of unspoiled wilderness beguiles Siberians into not being particularly concerned about the environment.

"In the winter a couple of hunters were surprised by a bear at night, right here in this camp," says Nikita. "One of the men was dragged out of his tent in his sleeping bag, but then the bear decided to go for the food supplies instead and vanished." Nikita prefers sleeping outside, but always has a knife and ax within reach. "Don't wake me up without a good reason, okay?" We decide to let Nikita sleep.

The second day has three very different phases for me. In the morning Chalka and I are suddenly a wondrous unit; we sweep through the steppes like the Lone Ranger and Silver, like Napoleon and Marengo, like Alexander the Great and Bucephalus. I think about opening a horse ranch in Altai: every morning Nadya would make buckwheat porridge and canned meat for breakfast while Chalka would neigh impatiently in the paddock, and at some point the *New York Times* would call and publish an interview titled "Drop-Out in the Altai Mountains: 'Horses taught me what's really important in life.'"

Two hours later my daydream is about a stack of ultra-soft down cushions. With them I could make the saddle, which has along the way transformed from leather to stone, into something reasonably bum-compatible.

By the afternoon I see myself in a doctor's consulting room; on the wall there are illuminated X-ray photos of my spinal column, one frontal, one lateral. In front of them stands an elderly gentleman in a white coat with an expression that even for a Russian would be considered deadly earnest.

Luckily it doesn't come to that; an hour later we reach our starting point. The animals appear bright and cheerful, the humans somewhat battered. "It was great, but—never again," says Galina. Yevgeni walked in front of his horse for the last mile because the jolting was causing him so much pain. Polya the Polo on a mogul-road is pure relaxation by comparison.

On the way back to Novosibirsk we listen to *The Miracle* by Queen and a miracle actually happens: Nadya and I are for the first time of the same opinion. "It was beautiful in Altai," she says. Then she puts her foot on the gas.

RELIGION REMIXED

IN **TIBET, PILGRIMS** circle Mount Kailash 108 times. In Japan they complete the 88-temple pilgrimage on the island of Shikoku. In Europe they tramp along the Way of Saint James to Santiago de Compostela with a scallop shell in their backpacks.

In Siberia, I take the 097C train to Krasnoyarsk (eleven hours, forty-two minutes), then the 124Ы to Kuragino (nine hours, fourteen minutes), and finally the 210 bus to Cherem-shanka (two hours); from there it is another twelve miles by car to Zharovsk, where my next host lives. And from his apartment a ten-mile walk to "Sun City." No one claimed the path to enlightenment was easy. At least on the way I have plenty of time to familiarize myself with *The Last Testament*, the transcript of all the wisdom and advice of the man I want to meet in deepest taiga.

"On the fourteenth day of January 1961 a predestined birth took place."[10] So begins the text about the former traffic cop Sergey Torop, now known as Vissarion. Sometimes in *The Last Testament* he is simply referred to as "The Word" or "The Truth."

He gathered five thousand followers who consider him to be the reincarnation of Jesus in five remote Siberian villages, one of which is Zharovsk.

In his texts I discover a passage that I like, as it seems to describe my long trek here. "When a traveler is being impeded by the load on his back, and the precipitous ravines with sharp hedges [sic], and stones flying upon him. All these obstacles have to be overcome by travelers along the roads of the Universe."[11]

The train to Kuragino takes more than nine hours to go a miserable 150 miles. *I shall overcome.* I arrive at four in the morning; I have to wait five hours for my connection. The ticket collector treats me as if I were trying to buy her six-year-old daughter rather than a ticket. *I shall overcome.* In the tiny café at the bus terminal the worst song in the world, "I'm a Gummy Bear," blares out of the owner's cell phone and her coffee tastes like Vegemite with sugar. *I shall overcome.* My host, Alex, a Vissarionite, had suggested a meeting place and knows my ETA but hasn't contacted me for days. *I shall overcome.*

Vissarion's doctrine is a kind of remix of the great world religions: Take charity and fear of the Apocalypse from Christianity, reincarnation from the Hindus, respect for all living creatures from Buddhism, and fatwa-like answers to everyday questions from Islam, then add a bit of hocus-pocus from esotericism and belief in extraterrestrial life from ufologists. And hey, presto! Thousands leave their old lives behind them, sell their houses and cars, move to Siberia, and join the community.

186   The underlying philosophy of a simple life in harmony with nature and the struggle against egotism for the good of the community makes this faith concept more mass-marketable than some others. Vissarion's followers submit to strict rules,

lead vegan lives, don't smoke or drink alcohol, and try to eat only what they can grow themselves. As much as possible they try to do without modern technology or money.

A self-sufficient community in the countryside that reflects the back-to-the-simple-life dreams of stressed-out city dwellers. With the addition of their own cohesive version of the Truth. Is it possible to get nearer to the current zeitgeist?

A B C
Okroshka • ОКРОШКА

Cold soup using kefir or kvass, a fermented bread beverage, as its basis. It usually contains cucumbers, potatoes, eggs, meat, and herbs. The French diplomat Eugène-Melchior de Vogüé was (unjustly) not a massive fan of this soup and, in the nineteenth century, compared it to the Russian soul: both are a mixture of tasty and disgusting ingredients. "Take a scoop of soup and you never know what will come out."

Shortly before my arrival at Cheremshanka, I finally receive a curt text message from Alex. It says: "White van."

The bus turns right at a sculpture with sun symbols and continues on to a neat village of wooden houses. On the lattice fencing there is a sign in colorful bubble letters: *There is no way to happiness.* Seeing me taking a photo of the sign, my seatmate says: "There used to be a second part to the message, which read *Happiness is the way.* Now they've built a shop there and that part of the fencing is missing. Too bad, isn't it?"

At the bus stop in fact there is a white four-wheel-drive Nissan. A small guy with long hair gets out, greets me, and introduces himself as Alex. Apart from his leather sandals he is dressed completely in white, including the baseball cap perched on his head. A woman in her early thirties sits in the passenger seat; she introduces herself as Minna from Finland.

We get in; Alex turns on the ignition and announces: "There are a few rules you need to know here." We rumble past the *There is no way to happiness* lettering, then proceed onto a dirt road toward the forest. "Firstly, never go alone into the taiga. It's not a normal forest. Many people have gotten lost there." He points to the thickly packed birch and larch trees all around us. "Secondly, you can stay for two or three days to relax. After that you have to help out. Thirdly, no alcohol, no cigarettes, no meat. Have you got a flashlight?" I have. "We don't have electricity at the moment, just a solar light in the kitchen. Cell phone reception is rare and then only in certain places in the village."

Soon the weather-beaten sign for Zharovsk can be seen poking out of the roadside grass. Alex parks on the main road outside a workshop. We walk through an impressive vegetable garden to a yellow wooden house that wouldn't look out of place in a catalog of Swedish vacation homes. It has an almost square front with four windows and a red chimney on the roof.

On the ground floor is the kitchen and living room, with a mattress for Minna. The fireplace was constructed by the man of the house, who is a bricklayer by trade but also works as an English teacher. Upstairs, accessible by a ladder, is Alex's bedroom, and a mattress has already been prepared for me in the corner.

The bookshelf survey: *Jane Eyre* by Charlotte Brontë, *Grimms' Fairy Tales*, a twenty-eight-volume encyclopedia. Next to them, some classroom editions of English-language classics: *Fahrenheit 451* by Bradbury, *The Letter* by W. Somerset Maugham, Orwell's *Animal Farm*.

There are a number of hardcover, gilt-embossed volumes of *The Last Testament* on a separate table next to a candle, a pendant with a golden cross, and a portrait of Vissarion. He looks astonishingly similar to Jesus, in the way he's commonly portrayed: a full beard; long, dark hair with a part in the middle; compassionate facial expression. In the photo of the Teacher, as they call him here, the radiant light blue of his eyes has something supernatural about it.

"Let Minna show you everything, I have to be off for two hours," says Alex, and then he leaves us alone.

She is also visiting here, but for a couple of months and already for the third time. "I'm writing a sociological/anthropological thesis on the role of faith in an isolated community," she says while mixing flour, eggs, and milk for pancakes. "It's pretty intense because in the process you're continually asking yourself the big questions. And always discussing what is right

189

and wrong. People say that a year here is like ten years in the world." The "world" is everywhere outside the five villages of the believers.

Minna has long brown hair, melancholic eyes, and sky-high ambitions: she wants to grasp the irrational using science, while fighting internal battles about which side she is more drawn toward—the spiritual or the empirical. She lived in Moscow for a couple of years, which is why she speaks Russian so well. In 2009 she saw Vissarion for the first time on a magazine cover. She was fascinated, "because he looked like a kids' movie version of Jesus."

Now she combines her own interests in the community with work. "You can forget time here; at some stage you just stop counting the days. But I can't take more than three months in one go. I get scared when talk turns to extraterrestrials, the Apocalypse, or negative energy."

She tells me of the early days of the community. On August 18, 1991, Vissarion appeared for the first time in public, one day before the putsch attempt in Moscow that was to mark the end of the Soviet Union. In those tumultuous times he offered followers a life under a kind of religious mini-communism in Siberia. "In 1993 he prophesied the Apocalypse would come in ten or at the most fifteen years. Only here, in the Siberian taiga, would people survive. There's a video of this prophecy, but now it's no longer recommended viewing."

I ask him how he managed to explain the absence of the Four Horsemen of the Apocalypse. "The Teacher says, 'Lying is allowed if it serves a greater cause.' His purpose was to bring as many people as possible to this community, which he achieved with this proclamation."

Truth No. 14:
Many politicians could learn from Vissarion.

He also managed to conjure up memories of groups like the Peoples Temple sect in Jonestown, where more than nine hundred people died in a mass murder–suicide. Toward the end of the '90s, voices critical of Jesus of Siberia began to rise on Russian TV and in newspaper reports. For members of the Orthodox Church he has roughly the same standing as the Scientology founder L. Ron Hubbard has with the Pope.

Preparations for Judgment Day continue to occupy Vissarion's followers. "I met a man in Petropavlovka who told me I had better hurry up with my thesis, as the world was going to end in 2016; Barack Obama would be the last U.S. president. He prophesized that an earthquake would hit Yellowstone Park and trigger a chain reaction."

Minna admits to being a bit bewildered. In the evenings she reads the Book of Revelation by candlelight, looking for parallels to what is happening here in Siberia. Many passages in her edition of the Bible are marked with a mauve highlighter.

She suggests visiting Sun City the next day and staying there for a couple of days. Vissarion lives in the holiest place of the community, on a hill. "There's always liturgy on Sundays. After liturgy, if the Teacher feels he is needed, he will answer questions. Maybe you want to know something from him?"

Well now, what do you ask Jesus? About the meaning of life? Which shares are about to go through the roof? Truthfully, which is better—Heaven or Hell? What really went on with Mary Magdalene? Does Crimea belong to Russia? Minna quickly brings me back to Earth: "Nowadays he only answers practical questions. The more concrete, the better. Sometimes it gets really absurd—people asking about the best way to clean shoes."

On the way here I discovered a similarly trivial passage in *The Last Testament*. To the question of whether it was a good or a bad sign when you attract mosquitoes, whether they prefer to bite the chaste or sinners, Vissarion answers: "Put yourself in the place of the mosquito. Would you make a dive for something if its consumption disgusted you?"[11]

Inwardly I rework my list of questions. It now consists of only one question: *How do you open a box of Cornflakes without wrecking the top flaps?*

TWO SEVENS
AND PLENTY OF
PUMPKINS

O**N A LITTLE** walk Minna shows me around the village, which lies between an impenetrable forest and the Kazyr River. One hundred fifty people live here and roughly 70 percent are Vissarion followers. Some of the wooden houses are well maintained, others are in need of repairs, and a few are not yet habitable. Some of the houses have unusually steep roofs so that in winter not much snow can gather there. It must be a paradise for children; there is a treetop walkway, a playground with *Masha and the Bear* figures, and an elaborate wrought-iron gate, above which stands the word *radost*—"joy." Opposite is the *teremok*, the communal building where discussions and choir practices take place, and there is a *banya*. For many people it's the best place to wash due to the lack of water pipes.

About two hundred yards outside the village there is a cemetery. On one of the gravestones, engraved in German, are the words *Glaube, Hoffnung, Liebe* ("faith, hope, love") next to an image of two praying hands. A fresh wreath of roses and pine branches are draped around a simple wooden cross. Minna explains that Alex's wife died a month ago. At sixty, she was seventeen years older than him. A tick bite was her downfall; she got encephalitis and fell into a coma. "No one here gets vaccinated," says Minna. "They believe God is taking care of them and if not then there's a reason behind it. But in summer the forest is full of ticks."

As far as illnesses are concerned, Vissarion is less than Jesus-like. "You are not allowed to heal an unbeliever; a believer doesn't need healing," he once said. He considers every form of suffering to be an indication of a punishment from God. If someone dies, mourning is not particularly excessive as the next reincarnation is bound to happen soon. Maybe I shouldn't ask him the Cornflakes question, but rather why am I suffering from backaches today.

On returning to the house I'm greeted in German by Tanya, a forty-seven-year-old linguist with laugh lines and a voice like a glockenspiel. She has been with the community for twenty-three years and has recently moved from Zharovsk to another village because she has just married. "I was brought here by heavenly powers—toward the Truth. So that I could translate the words," she says. "We followers of Vissarion are all predestined; I feel that in a previous life I was also a translator." Now she is translating *The Last Testament* into German; at the moment she is working on Chapter 10. "Vissarion has many German followers since a very good article about him appeared in GEO magazine in 2009," she says. She speaks without a hint of slang, never swallowing syllables, and formulates some sentences in a more complicated way than necessary, as only a keen language learner who hadn't lived in the corresponding country for long would do. "When were you born?" she asks. I tell her. "Libra is a good star sign. Like all the others. Can I do a few calculations?"

At that moment Alex returns. He says that the first frost could come that night and he has to pick the vegetables in the garden. I offer to help. "But only if you're not too tired!" A short while later we're hauling top-quality pumpkins to a wheelbarrow, in sizes ranging from soccer ball to airbag.

In the meantime Tanya picks tomatoes and analyzes my birth data. "You have got two sevens in your matrix; that means: you have a predestination," she announces. What are the names of your parents?" I tell her. She finds one of the names "beautiful" and the other "very beautiful" and reveals that I'm kind and determined and that I'm a sensitive sort of person. Almost as an aside she says that Minnichka, her nickname for Minna, "needs a good man who will stand by her for a long time." Then she returns to picking vegetables.

The next morning my alarm clock rings at five to four. I climb down the ladder to the kitchen and pack bread, fruit, raisins, and water in my backpack while Minna puts on the kettle. Half an hour later we set off; our headlamps are the only lights in the village. There is only one street, two possible directions: to the "world" or to the holy mountain where the Messiah lives, ten miles away. The service begins at eight. We can hope that one of the other followers will pick us up by car, but actually we both enjoy walking and the crisp morning air is refreshing. "It's like a pilgrimage," Minna remarks. "The hill where the service is taking place is at the easternmost point of all the settlements. After that there is four hundred miles of forest all the way to Lake Baikal."

The sun gradually rises; shafts of light break through the morning mist between the trees at the roadside, illuminating the fluffy seed hairs of cottonwood. I ask Minna whether she believes that Vissarion is the reincarnation of Jesus.

A B C

Putin Calendar 2017 • КАЛЕНДАРЬ ПУТИН 2017

With a print run of 200,000, this calendar contains two different facial expressions and the following images: Putin with candles. Putin with child. Putin with cat. Putin in a tree. Putin with veterans. Putin behind the wheel of something. Putin with amphora. Putin on a harvester. Putin in a delta wing plane beside a Eurasian crane. Putin on a horse. Putin as a fighter pilot. Putin with a wristwatch. Beneath the last picture there is a quotation: "Russia is a peace-loving, self-sufficient country. We do not need other people's territory or other people's resources. But if we are threatened we are prepared to use weapons to guarantee our security."

"I'm not a follower; sometimes it's all too much for me and I feel as if my head is going to explode if I don't leave immediately," she replies. Maybe she would have dropped her quest long ago were it not for the strange coincidences. For example, her last visit to Sun City a year ago: "On that particular day it was all too much. I was longing to speak to someone who was also having doubts, but there was no one. It's like a bubble here—hardly any other opinions penetrate it."

She began to let her imagination flow: if Vissarion really was who he claimed to be, he should give her a sign; otherwise she would leave the next day and return to her life, back in the "world." At first nothing happened. "A couple of minutes later I looked at my cell phone because I wanted to know the time. The display showed that there was a new message, which in itself is odd as we very rarely have reception here. The message read, and this is no joke: *Hello, it's me, Jesus.*" The message continued with sentences like: "If you disown me, I will disown you. If you accept me into your heart, I will be with you every day." The sender was a friend from Bremen who had herself just received the Biblical message from somebody else. "She told me later that she'd simply had a feeling that it would be good to send me that message."

Minna is receptive to symbols. Recently, when she was once again beset by doubts, a friend changed her two Facebook profile photos. The new main photo showed Lenin's hometown, Ulyanovsk; the smaller photo next to it was of Noah's ark. "I immediately understood the connection—Vissarion lived for a long time in Ulyanovsk and, by the way, considers Lenin to be the Antichrist. And the ark, of course, represents this place here."

Many of the followers speak of a kind of awakening. Some talk of just a "feeling of warmth" when they first arrived at Sun City. One woman told Minna that suddenly everything went black and she saw herself in Israel two thousand years ago. A man hiking in the snow in January claims to have heard an angel singing. "You could dismiss it as hogwash and craziness," says Minna. "But what I can't let go of is the thought that, supposing Jesus really came back to Earth, wouldn't it happen exactly as it's happening here?"

197

Only two cars pass us on the whole stretch, both fully laden. After some four hours we reach a wooden hut with glass windows that looks like a ticket booth. A man with long hair and a full beard sits inside the booth; he asks us who we are and whether we know the rules. On affirming, our names are handwritten onto a list; we walk a few yards further and are at the gate to Sun City. It consists of four wooden columns with a mobile of colored stones hanging in the middle and two mounted panels with aphorisms: *You shouldn't think about the support that you need, but who you can support* and *Not everyone who takes a step goes forward. Not everyone who stands still is without movement.*

I walk through the gate and try to feel something. No holy shakes, no singing angels. But the place does have a special aura through its spectacular setting. It has neat paths and gardens and dozens of wooden houses with pointed gables; the prettiest have roofs like magicians' hats and elaborately painted window shutters. The border to the east is a forested hill rising a few hundred meters above the settlement. If this really were the modern ark, the only thing remaining after the Apocalypse, then at least a really beautiful patch of the Earth would have been preserved.

A straight path leads to the gathering place where, on neatly trimmed grass, there is a roughly ten-foot-high beige sculpture: two angels back to back, above them a Vissarion cross inside a circle, and then a globe topped by a sun with fourteen rays.

Two men in white linen pants and white ponchos sit on a bench. "Don't walk over that area," warns Minna. "You're only supposed to do that when praying." One of the men greets us and Minna tells him we want to attend the service. He offers to accompany us there.

His name is Sasha, he has a full beard and noticeably strong hands—in the "world" he worked as a physiotherapist. He has lived in the region for thirteen years, seven of them in Sun

City. Only people who are particularly devout qualify to live here. The whole time we speak he has a pinecone attached to his hand, which he twists and twirls like a rosary.

I ask him what he finds hardest about living here, expecting complaints about the brutally cold winters, the isolation from the outside world, or the mosquitoes and ticks. His answer surprises me: "For the mind, the closeness of the Teacher is the hardest thing," he says. He is convinced that Vissarion can sense the vibes of his followers—the nearer they live to him, the more he senses. Every minor infringement of the rules, every impure thought causes strain, which, in turn, means negative energy that the Messiah apparently can feel.

We wind our way through the woods up the hill. Blue-berries grow on the side of the path; sometimes we hear the clear chime of a bell. Roughly halfway up the path there is a wooden throne, and above it an open parasol. "This is where

199

the Teacher answers questions after the service," says Minna. I imagine that it's something between the Sermon on the Mount and a call-in radio show.

A couple of hundred yards further on Sasha points to a simple wooden hut up in the woods. Every male member of the village retreats there twice a year for silent reflection, making wood carvings, and reading *The Last Testament*. For the entire three-day period there is a strict regimen of only seven hundred grams (about twenty-five ounces) of bread, plus tea, dried fruits, and onions.

Next to the path is a boulder that looks as if someone has scratched a cross on its surface. The followers consider it to be a sign of God. Sasha stops briefly and makes a sign of the cross in front of his chest—up, down, left, right, and then a circle as a symbol of the unity of the various religions.

The "Altar of the Earth" marks the highest point of a clearing. It consists of a wooden pavilion with various symbols of Christianity, Islam, Taoism, and Buddhism and a sculpture of dancing cherubs on the inside. The followers have gathered around it. The men are all wearing white linen clothing; the women are slightly more colorfully dressed, with long skirts and vests in pastel colors. Sasha points to a stone where we're supposed to sit and indicates that we should be quiet. With our totally different clothing we stand out like turkeys in a swan colony, but we attract barely more attention than the cold Siberian woodland air.

A priest in a red mantle says a few words, then the followers begin chanting. It's polyphonic and lofty, but also withdrawn, as if the participants were singing as softly as possible so as not to disturb the peace of Nature. For a moment I envision them standing right here singing their self-composed psalms while the rest of the world is being wiped out by volcanoes, earthquakes, and meteorites.

After the service, as the followers trudge gradually downhill, I ask Sasha why everyone wears white. "In earlier days the Teacher wore red; now he prefers white, which is why many followers believe it's the right color," he replies. On top of this, white represents purity and cleanliness.

After half an hour we reach the clearing with the throne. It is empty; today Vissarion doesn't consider it necessary to come. More than a hundred followers walk down to the meeting point in the center of the settlement to continue singing in a circle.

Like the sun rays, the fourteen roads of the village radiate from here in every direction. They have interesting names: Diamond Dust. Milky Way. Moonflowers. Children's Dreams. Crystal Gates. Wood Spirits. Silver Wells. Glistening Secrets. Starfield.

We turn onto Milky Way to visit a family that Minna got to know during her last visit: Yevgeni and Anastasia, with their two daughters, Bella, eight, and Sonya, three—a quartet of infectious happiness. The furnishing of their home is more comfortable and modern than I had imagined. There's a fridge, a stove, and computer, all powered by solar energy. Vissarion has slightly relaxed his previous aversion to technology and such comforts are no longer frowned upon. In the village there are a number of diesel generators that are used in the winter for heating.

We eat plums and drink herbal teas and chat about the potato harvest (quite good). Then I ask whether it would be possible to talk to Vissarion. "We'll call Vadim and see what happens," he says, reaching for a walkie-talkie. Vadim is the

201

evangelist; he has been recording every word of the Teacher for *The Last Testament* since 1992. A follower from the start and the only person in the community, apart from the Messiah, who is considered infallible. His answer, unfortunately, is only partially satisfying: Vissarion does not like talking to outsiders, but Vadim himself would be prepared to speak to me the next day.

Eight-year-old Bella accompanies us some of the way as we stroll in darkness to our accommodation. She proves to be a bright young lady with a fondness for precocious statements, issued in the casual manner of someone who never has doubts. "The age between three and four is particularly important for development," she says of her sister, and we discover from her: "Life in the village used to be much harder." Here you don't have to worry about kids going home alone and without flashlights. She is also certain about what she wants to be: "A confectioner at a bakery where none of the customers have to pay."

The guest accommodation resembles a simple backpack hostel: a large room with eight wooden bunk beds without mattresses. Men and women spend the night separate, in different buildings.

In the neighboring house there is a kind of canteen where two elderly ladies serve porridge for breakfast. There the next day we meet another guest, a businessman from Vladivostok who sells Japanese cars to New Zealand. The job, however, doesn't seem to qualify as his purpose in life. "I'm now looking for an ecovillage," he says. This is a trend in Russia: many people are leaving the cities because they realize that the part-time experience of nature in their dachas is not enough. Increasing numbers of people are joining the Anastasia movement, which propagates a sustainable life in nature. "I'm searching for a meaning in life and I haven't found it yet," he says. It reminds me of Sasha in Crimea and his admission, while gazing at shooting stars, that his generation is lacking a purpose. Can someone like Vissarion fill the gap?

In the meanwhile Minna is speaking to a man of around fifty who claims that he can read people. He sees "much light, many bright spaces, but also a dark space" in her and he would like to help her get rid of the dark space; he suggests a meeting with just the two of them. In his art of reading people he seems to be somewhat short-sighted: his head gets closer and closer to her head and his eyes don't break contact with hers, even for a millisecond. If we were being generous we could put this down to "keen focus," but it's probably more accurate to say he is ogling her.

We decide that this is probably a good time to leave; after all, we do have an appointment with the community's number two. Up to now I only know Vadim from an old music video of his band, Integral, featuring him sweeping across the dance floor to a disco beat with some pretty crazy, but at the same time acrobatic moves. Like a combination of Michael Jackson and a Cossack dancer, with the long hair of an '80s crooner.

We meet at a school on Starfield Street, some two hundred yards as the crow flies from Vissarion's house. Vadim's hairstyle has hardly changed since the video was made thirty years ago. A gray three-day beard and some wrinkles around his eyes are later additions. He radiates the deeply relaxed warmth of a person who is at ease with himself and the world and no longer has to dance around to be liked. "Ach, the music business," he says. "When you want to be successful, you have to go by the rules that the businesspeople make: they make you sing songs you don't like, to a public with simple tastes. You begin

203

lying to yourself. But life is too short to persist in a lie." After
five years as a professional musician he met Vissarion; soon he
became his most trusted right-hand man.

We go into the school building, a wooden house with three
classrooms and a kitchen. At the entrance there is a whole
range of colorful cross-country skis—soon it will be winter.
Vadim invites me to sit at the teacher's desk and settles in one
of the six pupil benches; the other way around would have
been more appropriate. There are math books on the shelf and
a poster with bright handprints of the schoolkids hangs on a
wall.

We talk about Sun City, about everyday life in seclusion,
and he outlines a utopia of contentment full of positive inter-
personal energy. "People here have escaped from the blind
alley into which society had maneuvered them because all

life, politics, and economics are corrupted by egotism. Here, however, the ego is considered the inner enemy that has to be tackled every day."

Linked to this is the idea of returning to the roles of men and women as they were in the time of Jesus. "When everyone has a role, there is no competition," says Vadim with his soft voice. "Women should serve men, but men should also serve women. A stable family is very important for society, but where can you still find that in Russia or Europe?"

At the very moment that the atheist Communism of Lenin and Marx ceased to exist in Russia, Vissarion brought into being a type of religious Communism as an experimental venture. The parallels are intriguing. The ideal is a life as laborer or farmer; all the harvest is shared, money should play no role, and status should be unimportant—apart from absolute obedience to the Teacher, of course. With his red book, Vissarion provides the ideological superstructure that enables his followers to believe they belong to a select circle that will survive the Apocalypse. According to Vadim, at the beginning of the '90s, particularly in Russia, the time was ripe, as people were emerging from a spiritual vacuum and many were yearning for a system they could believe in.

He has another piece of news for us: "Vissarion opened a Facebook account three weeks ago." For the first time in our conversation I get the feeling that Vadim doesn't totally agree with all of his boss's ideas. "Sometimes his actions are unpredictable. He just does what he feels to be right."

Now, at last, I know what these Siberian villages remind me of—a private Facebook group. All the people living here made a decision years ago to "like" Vissarion, thus signaling a readiness to accept his view of the world. And they "like" each other because all negative energy between them should be avoided. Sun City is an idyllic echo chamber deep in the taiga.

People live contentedly here in a filtered bubble where any information that contradicts Vissarion's doctrines is insignificant. No one checks facts, but when almost 100 percent of the people around you believe in something, it's easy to blank out first the counterarguments and then your own rationality. Putting it another way: things that five years previously you would have considered completely unthinkable are now upgraded to "possible." When so many people around me are convinced of it, then maybe there is something to it. Such a system can only work in isolation. Not everyone is convinced that they really are in the presence of the reincarnation of Jesus, but they at least believe that it's possible. A follower is not necessarily a believer but, in practice, there is no difference in loyalty.

ONE PHOTO TOO MANY

THE DENTIST AT Sun City is named Richard; he is thirty-seven and lives two doors away from the school. He has the same soft laugh as Vadim but he has dark eyes, a suntanned complexion, and short black hair. Richard shows us his practice. The equipment seems a bit primitive, but some things are still surprising to find in such a remote place: two sterilizers that look like microwave ovens, a formidable range of drills, an X-ray device that looks like a blow dryer and makes postage-stamp-sized images. When patients lie on the dental chair, which is upholstered in turquoise leather, they look directly at the benevolent, penetrating eyes of the Messiah and a sequence of numbers on the wall. 5148586. "My predecessor wrote those down, I have no idea what they mean," says Richard. The number 14 is considered holy as Vissarion was born on January 14.

I ask him whether he thinks a toothache is God's punishment. "It's all about streams of energy. If they aren't balanced, then you see the effects," he says. "But, of course, sugar is also to blame," he adds with a grin.

"What about serious illnesses?"

"The cause lies in the person; they are the result of not living a harmonious life," Richard believes.

We take a little walk, and he shows me the largest raspberries I've ever seen. They're almost egg-shaped and taste so sweet and delicious that for a second I wonder whether their proximity to his dental practice is part of the business model. Of course, that's nonsense, because treatment is free of charge for all villagers.

At the upper end of the road, a new communal house, from which you can survey the whole village, is being built for meetings. It has a big, rounded window, which from farther away looks like a huge eye. Next to this house there is a path laid with expensive flagstones leading up to Vissarion's house.

"What's it like living so close to the Master?"

"We describe it jokingly like this: Below in the village the people are in boiling water; up here we are on the grill," Richard answers. But the houses up here are visibly larger and of a higher quality; it seems like the posh area of Sun City.

Now I make a mistake. I reach for my camera, watching Richard's reaction in case photography is not allowed here.

But he doesn't seem to have any objections, so I snap a shot of Vissarion's house. White stone walls, a rounded portal, two statues of cranes in the neatly trimmed garden. Not a palace, but it is a pretty little villa.

As we make our way back a man approaches us from behind. He seems to be angry and demands that I delete the photo immediately. I comply and he lets us continue.

Back at the entrance gate of the village we are again accosted. A bearded guy wearing the usual linen clothes asks us what we were thought we were doing taking photos. How did he know? The lines of communication seem to work better than I had imagined. He also wants to know why he wasn't informed of our presence, as he is the guest-minder here, and how we managed to meet up with Vadim. His tone is calm—watch out for those negative vibes—but his physical tension betrays his anger. Minna tries to pacify him and says that we registered on arrival.

"How did you get here in the first place?" he asks in a milder tone.

"By walking from Zharovsk." This seems to be unusual, which makes us even more suspect.

Once we assure him that we were planning to leave Sun City today, he lets us go. We return to our accommodation to gather our belongings. On entering the dining area we sense a change in mood, though the faces show no sign of negative emotion. "What, you're still here?" says a woman with a friendly smile.

AFTER WALKING A few hours we're back at Alex's house; a fire flickers in the living-room fireplace. I ask him what he thinks about my photo faux pas. "Not such a big problem; they'll soon calm down." He knows what it's like to run afoul of Vissarion's rules. Alex runs a shop on the main road that sells a wide variety of goods and has a small DVD rental section—mostly dealing in action movies, at ten rubles per DVD. A number of followers found this a bit disconcerting and asked for Vissarion's view during one of the Sunday question-time sessions. The answer was that it was not okay and Alex was expelled from the "united families," the group of particularly compliant devotees. Alex still rents out DVDs.

He is, in fact, worried about the lack of entertainment in the village; he has an eighteen-year-old son. Alex shows me a rough design for a café that he is planning to open in a few years, with guest beds and a stage for concerts. On the weekends there could be a disco, and in the small tower a telescope for observing the stars.

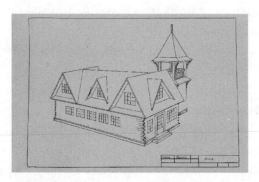

Despite the limited cultural life, Alex still thinks Zharovsk is a paradise in comparison to other villages of similar size. "Many Russian villages are almost completely destroyed. By drugs and alcohol. Particularly in the central regions of the country," he says. "Do you want to know the truth about Russia?"

"Sure," I say, "that's why I came here."

He tells me a joke: "A tribe of Indians captures a Russian, a Frenchman, and a German. The chieftain gives each of them two steel balls. He tells them, 'Whoever does something with these balls that I find interesting goes free. The others will be killed.' The next day he goes first to the German, who balances both balls on the tips of his fingers: 'Look! That's German precision.' Next, the Frenchman shows him how good he is at juggling. Finally it's the Russian's turn: he has lost one ball and damaged the other. The chieftain can't believe his eyes and sets him free."

Alex thinks that tells you everything about Russians. "My son's just like that. When he was three or four we let him go alone to the village. One hour later he came back; he had somehow lost all his clothes and was completely naked. Recently I lent him two modems; the next day he returned only one of them. He bought himself an amp—the next day it was kaput. Now he's building a house." Well, that's going to be fun, I think to myself.

While we're on the subject of Russia: "What is Putin actually like?" I ask Alex.

"The country is huge; we need a king, a strong leader. He is liked because he's a patriot, not a thief, and he doesn't drink. And he gives people money for a second child."

I sense that he doesn't really mean "he is liked" but rather "I like him." But during my travels here I often have the impression that people are somewhat more cautious about praising Putin because of my roots, because they know how critically their leader is viewed in the West.

I only see Vissarion again in a few video clips on Alex's computer. His sublime presence evokes a historical film version of

Jesus. "It is wrong to come to conclusions without knowledge," he decrees in a solemn voice, and the followers adoringly nod. When he's right, he's right.

Truth No. 15:
The greater your charisma, the wiser you will seem when stating very simple truths.

KYZYL

Population: 110,000

Federal District: Siberia

GOING TO PUTIN'S

I HAVE TO GET back to the "world." Leaving is difficult; the simple life in the country has been like a short vacation. Even though (or maybe because) I received no feeling of enlightenment—not even two sevens in the matrix could help me there.

I've arranged to meet someone in Kyzyl about whom I know nothing other than that his online profile shows Putin in a black suit, casually walking away from a burning White House. His short answer to my couch request was a single line: "*Privyet*. I have a place where you can spend a couple of nights," and his telephone number. He asks me via text message whether it's okay for me to stay in a completely empty apartment that's up for sale. Of course, I write back. I don't even know his name.

I know a little bit more about the region he lives in. It seems to have little in common with the peaceful altruism of the place I've just left. *Lonely Planet* warns of being out on the streets of Kyzyl after dark because of the numbers of drunks out and about who, apparently, are inclined to be violent.

This is doubly threatening as the most popular local sport is wrestling. Additionally, shamanism is in fashion, so the vodka-crazed fighting machines, before leaving me half-dead on the sidewalk, will rip out some of my hair to make an effigy. Even years later, long after the broken ribs from the suplex slam have healed, they could cause me horrific pains with the help of that effigy. Or so I imagine.

A B C
Queer • ГОМОСЕКСУАЛИСТ

Having a non-traditional sexual orientation, which in Russia was only removed from the list of mental illnesses in 1999 and is still considered "treatable." Since 2013 it has been an offence to speak positively about homosexuality to minors. The 2014 Eurovision Song Contest, won by the bearded drag performer Conchita Wurst, was a major educational challenge for families gathered around their TV sets. "There is no limit to our outrage. It is the end of Europe. There are no more men or women in Europe, just it," raged Vladimir Zhirinovsky, the leader of the ultranationalist party LDPR, who is well known for provocative sound bites. However, "outrage" was a bit of an exaggeration, at least if he thought he was speaking for the whole country. At the voting stage, Wurst received a highly respectable eight points from callers in Russia.

214

To get to Kyzyl I use the online ridesharing platform Bla-BlaCar. In this instance the "car" part is accurate; not, however,

the "blabla." The driver bears an uncanny resemblance to Burt
Reynolds and his son looks like Andre Agassi. Neither of them
seem to feel any need to communicate. We hardly speak on
the five-hour journey. In between the cell phone dead zones, I
try to plan the next stage of my travels, an activity with quite a
high potential for frustration in Russia.

The direct flight from Kyzyl to Irkutsk, near Lake Baikal,
which would have taken two hours, is no longer available. The
next one is in a week, which is too late for me, so I have to
switch to bus and train.

In Western Europe we're used to road and rail networks
that spread across all countries. Consequently there's always
a relatively direct way to get from A to B. In Russia it's different. Here there are dead ends: one way leads there, and the only
option is the same way back. Because of an obtrusive mountain range, to get to Irkutsk from Kyzyl by the overland route
is like wanting to travel from New York City to Washington
only to discover that there's no direct way and you can only go
via Toronto.

So I have to go five hundred miles by bus back to Krasnoyarsk (fourteen hours); from there I can get a flight to spare
me from sitting on a train for an additional seventeen hours.
At such times you begin to understand how big Russia really
is. On the map the distances don't appear to be particularly
impressive.

Outside, dusk is falling. Burt Reynolds is driving like he's in
a live remake of The Cannonball Run. He takes the normal bends
at seventy-five miles per hour, the sharp ones at sixty. He
doesn't seem to have any problems with coordination, as he
is able to simultaneously smoke an Optima cigarette and type
a message into his cell phone. When we reach Kyzyl in total

215

darkness, I show the driver the address on Maps.me—Friendship Street 1, Apartment 77.

Naturally, I keenly observe the characters out and about on the streets. Shortly before our stop, I do indeed see a man lurching heavily and holding a bottle. I'm relieved that Reynolds drops me right in front of the door.

I thank him and call my host, who comes to the door. At last, a Russian in track pants. He has short black hair and Asian features. "Hi, I'm Yevgeni. Did you have a good trip? Here is the key," he says, then quickly shows me around the three-room apartment on the second floor. No furniture, no kitchenette; two pine twigs next to the bathtub provide the only decoration. I feel more like a real estate buyer than a guest. "I have to go, maybe we could meet up tomorrow," says Yevgeni.

And then I have an empty apartment all to myself. What I don't have is a mattress, drinking water, or, apart from a few pine nuts, food. On the way here it didn't look as if there were any shops open or even a takeout place in the vicinity. It's irrelevant anyway, as I wouldn't have dared leave the apartment on account of the drunken wrestling shamans. I spread out my thin sleeping bag on the parquet floor, fold my winter jacket into a pillow, and wait for daylight.

IN THE CENTER of Kyzyl three metal lions bear a globe out of which a colossal hairpin reaches for the sky. At its tip is a balancing stag. The fifty-five-foot-high monument is supposed to mark the central point of Asia; God knows how they figured that out. A place near Ürümqi in China, roughly 1,250 miles south of Kyzyl, also claims to be the center of Asia. The statue there, also featuring a globe, is sixty feet high, which doesn't necessarily mean the supporting calculations are more precise.

If you were to commission a hundred geospacial experts to come up with more accurate coordinates, there would probably be another hundred globe monuments scattered across the landscape.

Truth No. 16:
Geography is sometimes a matter of opinion.

Central point or not, I enjoy simply being a tourist for a day and just drifting around. To begin with I treat myself to an overdose of cookies in a "time café," where customers pay not for what they consume but for the amount of time they spend there. In the cultural center, four musicians, named Mengi, Mergen-Cherel, Ayas, and Zhonchalay, are holding a concert featuring traditional instruments and throat singing. If you were previously unaware that human vocal cords can produce a sound resembling a didgeridoo, you must stop what you're doing immediately and give throat singers a listen. In a moment of sheer enthusiasm I almost buy a *doshpuluur*, a three-stringed lute, with the carved head of a horse at the end of the neck and a sound box covered with goatskin. Unfortunately it won't fit in my backpack.

What I also would really like to take home is some Scythian gold from the National Museum. A number of years ago a German–Russian team of archaeologists made a sensational discovery as they were excavating the royal kurgan burial site Arzhan II. They hit upon six thousand pieces of jewelry and mini sculptures made of gold: bracelets, necklaces, and a whole army of tiny panthers that served as garment ornaments. The most valuable artifacts are kept in a separate room behind a guarded armored door. My favorite pieces are the small stags, with their huge antlers and stumpy tails—2,500 years old and still pretty cute.

My phantomlike host doesn't contact me (I do actually meet him once more, for one minute when I give him back the key before my departure). So I meet up with Ayu, someone I had also gotten in touch with before my arrival. We meet at 7:30 PM and it's already dark.

Ayu is twenty-four, has long, dark hair, and is wearing a white blazer, a blouse with a floral pattern, and brand-new sneakers. She arrives with her mother, who is also very nice, but who leaves after five minutes. I conclude that I must not look like an ax murderer (too bad, actually, because if I did I would be able to scare the hell out of the local ultraviolent wrestlers. On the other hand, realistically, at this time of day they're so drunk they wouldn't know the difference anyway, and on top of that, the street we're on is pretty dark).

I ask Ayu, who is a petite woman, how she has the courage to be out on the streets this late. "The only thing the drunks want from me is money for alcohol," she says cheerfully. "I've never had a problem, even walking home at two in the morning." She actually lives in Poznań, Poland, where she is studying Turkology, but returns home during the semester breaks to visit her family. She speaks fluent English, Polish, Russian, Mongolian, and Tuvan; she thinks quickly but walks slowly, speaks softly but sometimes with anger.

"We are victims of Russian propaganda that makes everything that happens in Tuva sound bad," she rails. "If someone from Tuva commits murder they say, 'Tuvan man commits murder.' If a Russian commits murder in Tuva, then they say, 'Murder in Tuva' without naming the perp's country. Sometimes they simply dig up old murder stories and circulate them again a couple of months later." She makes the distinction customary in these parts of the country—"Russian" means the Slavs, and the minorities are called Chechens, Tuvans, or Yakuts, although, of course, on their passports they are equally Russian. "If I said that I come from Tuva and I have a knife in my pocket, people would immediately believe me," says Ayu. "And if I said I own twenty reindeers, they'd believe that too. A lot of people's perceptions have nothing to do with reality." However, the times from which these impressions originate are not too long ago. Her grandma, whom she visited that afternoon, used to live as a nomad.

For a drunk's next step, all four directions are equally mathematically probable. A dark figure fitting this description approaches us on the sidewalk. Ayu suggests crossing to the other side of the road. "Alcohol is a problem here; people become drunk more quickly for genetic reasons," she says. The guy staggers away.

A B C

Russian Squat

A squatting position radiating nonchalance in which the upper arms rest on the knee while you gaze seriously into the distance. The body language is reminiscent of hip-hop record covers of the '90s or shitting in the woods. Suitable paraphernalia includes track pants and bling. Early in 2016 there was a short trend of posting photos of the Russian squat on Facebook and Instagram, but after two weeks the fashion was over, which was one of the better pieces of news in 2016.

I ask her about the reasons behind the propaganda against her minority. "After the collapse of the Soviet Union we wanted independence, but Moscow didn't approve," she replies. The powers that be like to flex their muscles here. Like this afternoon. She wanted to attend a Buddhist lecture on altruism, but the Tibetan guest speaker was arrested shortly beforehand. Why he was arrested remains a mystery.

For our evening meal we go to a self-service canteen called Vostok, which is well hidden on the second floor above a supermarket and which I never would have discovered alone. The *pelmeni*, dumplings with sour cream, taste fantastic and cost virtually nothing. It's always a pleasure to go with locals to their favorite places.

Back on the street we talk about Schopenhauer and Thomas Mann, about *The Tin Drum* and Wagner, about Berlin and Dresden. Ayu plans to take some German lessons soon, but she already seems to know more about the country's culture than most Germans of her age.

"I have a couple of friends in Berlin. There, I like a lot that people who make an effort to become integrated are accepted. Russia, on the other hand, is pretty racist—especially in Saint Petersburg and Moscow."

The street is gloomy, the asphalt uneven and full of cracks—there are often earthquakes here. There are no streetlights; the only light comes from a few windows. Every now and then a barking dog runs up to us; sometimes we come across men tottering in an uncoordinated manner. But no one bothers us, and eventually we say our goodbyes and catch cabs home. The drunken wrestlers must be elsewhere tonight.

OLKHON ISLAND

Population: 1,500

Federal District: Siberia

OLKHON SHOKOGUN

OLKHON ISLAND IN Lake Baikal is the destination I've been most eagerly looking forward to visiting. My private dacha owner, Yevgeni in Novosibirsk, went into rhapsodies about the hiking opportunities there, the photos of the region look stunning, and my host there, Sergei, appears to be particularly interesting—a former investment banker who gave up his job to build an Orthodox church in the village of Khuzhir, where he now rings the bell every day. He also invites large numbers of guests to stay without charge in his self-built wooden house. His story is so inspiring that there are articles about him in the international press. A friend who had been to Olkhon told me of his meeting with Sergei with a glint in his eye.

Unfortunately, one of the cast-iron laws of travel is that it's precisely the place of which you have the highest expectations that has the greatest potential to disappoint. Like the Paris syndrome (in Japanese: *Pari shōkōgun*), which describes a heavy depression that affects Asian travelers to France who expect the city of love to be oozing in romance, full of gorgeous women wearing Louis Vuitton dresses and humming Édith Piaf melodies from dawn till dusk, only to discover that it stinks of urine and tourist groups are not greeted with open arms.

The journey from Irkutsk takes six hours in a minibus, the interior of which is skillfully padded with foam so the roof and sides resemble a recording studio. Further clues to the driving style and the quality of the road are provided by the many cracks and small holes in the windshield and the multitude of saint figurines dangling below the rearview mirror.

A B C

@Sputnik_Not

A Twitter account that, with pitch-black humor, pokes fun at Russia, its propaganda, and at "Russia's" American president, Donald Trump. It displays photos or short videos with titles like "Putin: Russia against censorship outside Russia," "Russians are safe from invading NATO forces" (the photo shows vehicles stuck in deep mud), or "Putin: Russia is investing heavily in hi-tech products, e.g., cereals." The platform has more than fourteen thousand followers, nearly a tenth of the number that follow the original *Sputnik*.

A small car ferry transports the bus across the deepest lake in the world; the water is a vibrant turquoise and the sky slightly cloudy. My first impression of Olkhon is that its greenish-yellow hills and happy cows remind me of the Shetland Islands.

The good news is that the dirt road to Khuzhir is rough, but less rough than I expected. The bad news is that Sergei is not there. "He's in France at the moment," says a young man, who is presumably his son, as I arrive at the address Sergei had sent me when he confirmed my couchsurfing request. It's great that he offers me accommodation in his absence, but a pity that I can't meet him personally.

There's a mattress prepared for me in an army tent of about 130 square feet pitched on a green area next to the church. It smells of methylated spirits and instant noodles, and apart from me there are a travel blogger couple from Finland, a geologist from France, and three Russian backpackers. There's room for all on other mattresses in the tent.

In the local corner shop, I witness the attempts of a group of Chinese tourists to explain to the vendor that one of them doesn't want to buy all of the specially priced pack of four fruit yogurts, but only a single one. This leads to considerable communication difficulties: the grumpy lady at the counter doesn't want to split the product; the customers don't understand why. Paris syndrome in the house?

The majority of visitors to the island come from China, which is astonishing as the island doesn't fit the usual criteria for vacation destinations. Tourist research surveys claim that the vacationing Chinese are mostly interested in luxury stores, high-class hotels, and good wireless reception. You can forget about all of these in the dusty Wild West town of Khuzhir; most of the guest rooms don't even come with a shower. "But in all our schoolbooks they tell us that Lake Baikal is beautiful," a tourist from Chengdu tells me, adding: "And there's a popular Chinese song about it, too." Investors have already noticed the potential; on the southern shores of the lake, at Baykalsk, there are plans for a modern tourist paradise specifically tailored to the needs of guests from the Far East. A pool of Chinese companies headed by Chungjingxin are planning to invest an incredible US$12 billion in the project; this amounts to twice the cost of building Disneyland in Shanghai.

At sunset, everyone gathers for the photo op at Skala Shamanka, a craggy rock extending into the lake that local shamans believe to be the home of the god Khan Gutababai. They've decorated a number of poles with colorful materials to make things a bit prettier for the holy resident. They say that people who come here should only have clear and positive thoughts, because everything is amplified here. Well, that's *really* great; I'm still annoyed about missing Sergei.

At least I've arranged a meeting tomorrow at midday with Russia's most famous shaman to learn something about his healing powers, his excursions to other worlds, and the legends of Olkhon Island. He's called Valentin Khagdaev and he seems to be a sort of household shaman of the rich and powerful. According to his website, he looks into the future for the supermodel Natalia Vodianova and helped the pop singer Dima Bilan win the Eurovision Song Contest in 2008. And, of course, he has shaken hands with Putin. In the Soviet Union times shamanism was demonized and persecuted, but now it's becoming more and more popular in Russia. In Buryatia, the province on the eastern shores of Lake Baikal, the practices of traditional healers are even recognized by the health authorities.

OLKHON IS FORTY-FIVE miles long and eight miles wide, making it the fourth-biggest lake island in the world. If you believe the shamanistic tales, a whole horde of spirits live here, next to which all the elves of Iceland would look like kids in sheets at a fancy-dress party.

A perplexing peculiarity of the island is its stillness. If you walk along the sandy beach directly at the waterline you can hear the sounds of water, but only ten or fifteen feet inland it's suddenly completely quiet. The view to the rounded cliffs on the mainland, often cloaked in mist, is also magical. And finally, the fantastic taste of cold smoked omul, a member of the salmon family that only swims in Lake Baikal, can only be explained by magic.

The next morning I call the über-shaman to arrange a meeting place. He is inconsolable—he had totally forgotten about our meeting, is now on a ship, and wouldn't be returning to Olkhon in the foreseeable future. Dammit! What have the island spirits got against me?

A B C
Tyutchev, Fyodor • ТЮТЧЕВ, ФЁДОР

Nineteenth-century poet who succeeded in making himself immortal with four lines. Every Russian knows them, and seldom has a national mythos been better described. A rough translation goes something like this: "Russia cannot be understood with the mind alone, / No ordinary yardstick can span her greatness: / She stands alone unique— / In Russia one can only believe."[13]

I'm a bit stubborn; I don't give up easily. At Nikita's Homestead, Olkhon's most famous lodgings, I ask the receptionist whether she can recommend a shaman, telling her that it's urgent. The woman behind the desk looks at me a bit pityingly, probably puzzling over which horrifying illness I'm seeking to have driven out. "I think one lives at the end of the road, Valentin. The house with the blue fence; you can't miss it," she says. Apparently all shamans are called Valentin.

I go there and knock on the garden door. A young woman comes to the door and I give her the name of the man I'm looking for. She goes into the house, and a short while later, a colorful, elflike figure with a carved walking stick greets me. His outfit consists of suit pants and polished patent leather shoes, a kind of Hawaiian shirt, and a stone necklace with a feather in it. He is about four foot nine and has a wrinkly face full of wisdom, glittering gold teeth, and spritely but slightly startled-looking, penetrating eyes.

Bull's-eye, I think, and explain the reason for my visit. His answer is somehow superb and poetic, because seldom have the opposites of perception and truth, of projection and reality, been put so succinctly. At the same time it is horribly disappointing. "I'm not a shaman," he says. "I'm just very, very old."

I give up. Screw Olkhon. In the afternoon I catch the next ferry and leave the island.

Truth No. 17:
Just because every other tourist loves a place, it doesn't necessarily mean you'll have a good time there.

A HECTARE
OF HOPE

MAYBE ANGELA MERKEL sometimes sits, deep in thought, in her office on the seventh floor of the chancellery, gazing out at the Brandenburg Gate and the parliament building, and asks herself why this Vladimir Putin character is so popular in his country. She could find a possible answer in the Sakha Republic: gifts. There, at the moment, you can get a hectare of land—about two and a half acres—completely free. "A good idea," thinks Kirill, who has just sent off his online application. He lives in Yakutsk, a thousand miles northeast of Olkhon. "There is so much spare land here. My grandma used to tell us that during the Soviet times there were more cows and horses than people in this region. Sakha has a huge potential."

Kirill is twenty-six and works as a wedding photographer and video producer. Though he would have preferred to have been a rock star with his heavy metal band Narchim—the name means "ice sword." Kirill lives with Anya, Wanya, and

Bella: his wife is twenty-two, their son one and a half, and the dog is an extrovert chow chow.

"You can also give the passport details of your parents and grandparents on the application to get even more hectares," he explains. The only catch is that after five years they check whether the land really is being developed and used. If not, it returns to the state. The Ministry of Development of the Far East even has a few suggestions—you could grow strawberries, breed goats or rabbits, start a project linked to tourism, or build up a hunting business. As Sakha is renowned for its subterranean diamond deposits, there is one restriction: mining for natural resources in Russia is the privilege of the state.

In the summer there was a false report in the British tabloid *Daily Express* claiming that British subjects could also apply for pieces of land there. Accompanying the article were spectacular pictures of mountains and bears that looked so inviting that of the fifty thousand participants in a reader's poll, forty thousand could imagine moving to eastern Russia.

In actual fact the offer was initially only for people from Sakha and the neighboring regions, and a few months later it was extended to include other Russians. "We're afraid that the Chinese will try to get a lot of land," says Kirill. "Actually, that's not the plan, but there's so much corruption here." He could imagine starting up a farmstead. Selling milk, meat, and cream. One of his uncles earns his living this way and he could learn a lot from him.

There's no lack of space in the region. Sakha is almost as big as India, but has a population of less than half a million. The reason for this is not only the poor infrastructure but also the extremely harsh winters. Temperatures of minus forty or fifty degrees Fahrenheit are not unusual. It's so cold that people

229

keep their small children indoors in December and January, they can't wear glasses outdoors because they freeze to the skin, and they leave car motors running all night to be able to use them the next day (unless they have heated garages and wrap up the batteries in warm blankets). All buildings in Sakha are on stilts because otherwise the heat from the houses would melt the permafrost, which is bad for the foundations. You can often take shortcuts by walking under a high-rise building.

A B C

Underpass • ПОДЗЕМНЫЙ ПЕРЕХОД

A tunnel beneath a large road in a city; well worth using, as crossing a road during rush hour can be lethal. There are sometimes interesting opportunities for shopping as well: you can buy fake university diplomas, health certificates, and pirated DVDs. Nowadays these commodities can only be found in the outskirts of larger cities, as selling has been curbed in the central areas.

"It is winter here for nine months and summer for three," says Kirill's mother, Lyuba. We visit her in the somewhat run-down village of Oy, which translates to "ouch" and is full of wooden houses, some forty miles from the city. Car wrecks litter the side of the gravel road, and at the entrance to the village, the tanks of an abandoned dairy rust away. There is no sewage system; the expense of installing a facility that could withstand extreme frost would be too great. Instead every household has an outhouse in the garden. The surroundings consist of

A statue of Lenin in the Altai Republic. In the center of almost every Russian city there is a monument to the über-revolutionary.

I spent eight days traveling through the Altai Republic with Nadya—
our rented car had to endure a lot.

Accommodation in Aktash. It took time to adjust to the diversity
of visual attractions in the room.

In the southern Altai Republic you can come across wild camels.
It's only a few miles from here to the Mongolian border.

The guide at the Roerich Museum. The much-traveled landscape
painter liked using vibrant colors.

Vissarion's church in Siberia. The leader of the sect claims to be the reincarnation of Jesus.

He managed to gather a following of some five thousand believers. Every Sunday they celebrate a service lasting several hours in "Sun City."

Minna from Finland was writing her thesis on the religious community and spending a couple of months in Siberia.

Statues of riders in Kyzyl. Scythian heritage shapes the city's culture. A site with finds of priceless gold figurines is nearby.

A concert for the "Followers." My host, Alex (left), organized a show in the community hall of the village of Zharovsk.

Olkhon Island in Lake Baikal. Shamans have decorated wooden posts with colorful ribbons.

The village of Khuzhir is becoming a popular tourist destination, but parts of it are a bit run-down.

The Skala Shamanka is the most famous landmark on Olkhon. The local shamans believe it to be the home of the god Khan Gutababai.

Couchsurfer Kirill (middle) with family. He dreams of soon having his own parcel of land in Yakutsk.

The harsh winters in Yakutsk are particularly difficult for children. The youngest ones are often confined to the apartment for weeks during the coldest months.

Commemorating the Great Patriotic War. There are memorials everywhere: in the Altai Republic ...

... Volgograd ...

... Elista ...

... and Mirny.

A statue of Lenin in Mirny in an unusual pose.

A gigantic crater with a viewing platform. Locals have nicknamed the disused diamond mine the "asshole of the world."

Thanks to warmhearted people like Igor, Marina, and Juliya (left to right) I got to know Russia not as a lone tourist, but as if I were visiting good friends.

A sculpture recalls the discovery of the diamond mine, with a reindeer breeder leading geologists to the site.

In Mirny I stayed in teachers' accommodation. An impromptu party in the neighboring room.

A political statement: "We're still a bit Communist here," said Marina.

The houses in Mirny are pretty drab; the playgrounds, on the other hand, are more colorful.

Russians sure know how to party. Above: the owners of a bar in
Khabarovsk. Below: a couchsurfer meet-up in a *banya* in Vladivostok.

endless forests and barren, fallow land; new landowners can't expect an easy life here. "But in return, we don't suffer from natural catastrophes—no earthquakes," says Lyuba, a cheerful retired nurse who has short, brownish-red-dyed hair and wears a flowery patterned top.

She doesn't care who governs in Moscow; the capital is six time zones away. Then she tots up the reasons she is content with her life out here: "I get a pension of 20,000 rubles a month"—around US$320—"and my husband and mother do too. Gas in winter costs 12,000 rubles a month, plus we pay for electricity, but there are few other expenses. We grow almost everything in the garden, my husband doesn't smoke or drink, so we manage just fine. Guess what! My second son smokes, although he's a surgeon. He really should know better, but he blames stress. Can you come back on Saturday for the potato harvest?"

"I'd love to, but I'll be in Mirny by then."

"Pity. By the way, the most beautiful women come from Vladivostok!"

"Great! I'll be there in ten days."

On the return journey Kirill says that visiting home always reminds him of World of Warcraft.

"There's a place at the beginning where the hero tanks up on energy. It's exactly the same for me in Oy."

Maybe he and his small family will soon have their own loading unit, on his own hectare of land somewhere in the cold expanses of Sakha, with Anya, Wanya, and the dog.

DIAMONDS

THERE ARE TWO natural injustices in the world: beauty and natural resources. People with symmetrical faces don't have to try as hard to be liked. Countries with oil and gas don't have to be as innovative to become rich.

If you combine beauty and resources, you end up with diamonds. When you look at a diamond mine you can see that everything has its price; there's always a balance. For example, in Mirny: people seeking beauty (in this case, glittering stones) have to accept ugliness (in this case, a huge, gaping hole in the ground).

In a general store in the small town they sell souvenir plates with pictures of the "asshole of the world." To make the finished article optically tolerable the artist has painted a yellow bird, a church, and a bowl full of diamonds around the rim. Small plates cost 500 rubles, the larger ones 800. They don't sell particularly well, the owner tells me.

The day after my arrival in Mirny I meet the director of the Department of Youth and Culture in the library. Her name is

Marina; she has black, curly hair and black eyes, both inherited from her parents, who come from Azerbaijan and Georgia. A round pendant hangs from her neck with *Forever Young* written on it; at twenty-three, she is pretty young for her impressive job title.

Today, however, she is pursuing even greater ambitions: to be a film star. The Italian director Saverio Pesapane is holding an audition as he's planning to film in Mirny with grant funds from the Venice Film Festival. The screenplay is about a young man who wants to leave the city for good; he has already bought his plane ticket. Then strange things start to happen, which could be taken as omens that maybe he should remain where he is. A mysterious shaman in the snow plays a significant role, and in the encounters between them, viewers have to puzzle out what is reality and what is illusion.

Eight people have come to the audition: seven men and Marina. I think her chances are good, and not only because she is the only woman among the applicants. Her personality seems to be eminently suited to the performing arts: she's a feisty woman with plenty of bounce who always speaks and laughs a little bit louder than necessary, as is often true of people on the smaller side.

Marina is called into an adjoining room; the door is between two metal bookshelves, one labeled "New Books" and the other "Russian Literature."

I get into a conversation with two young men with short, practical hairstyles who have hooked their thumbs in the pockets of their jeans, which always looks less casual than it's supposed to. They say that Mirny is pretty boring after a while for people of their age. There are only two places to go dancing—Malibu, where there's a fight almost every night, and The Globe, where it's a bit quieter. To make up for this, there is plenty of good hunting to be had in the surrounding forests—elk, reindeer, geese, and ducks. A couple of days ago, however, a hunter was killed by a bear, which happens from time to time.

Marina comes back. "It went well," she beams. "The director wanted to know lots about my training and about the city." She found it very interesting what he said about his choice of location: "You live here in a unique place, far away from the rest of the world, with this huge hole in the ground. Maybe someone who comes from somewhere else can better appreciate this peculiarity and see something in Mirny that you don't see."

On a tour of the city I have the opportunity to test this statement. And today is a special day, as Russia is voting for a new parliament. Loudspeakers on the lampposts are playing patriotic songs to get people in the mood. The songs are about Russia's greatness and heroes of the Great Patriotic War. "I was woken by them this morning," says Marina. "I hate these songs, although I'm a patriot. Why can't they play Justin Bieber or OneRepublic?"

In the main square we walk past a statue of Lenin. The Communist hero is part of every cityscape; there are more than five thousand registered statues and busts of him. Something or other is wrong about this particular one, but I can't quite put my finger on it.

A B C

Vk.com • ВКОНТАКТЕ

The most important social network in the country, with 100 million active members. Visually and functionally it's almost identical to Facebook circa 2006; nevertheless the clone is considerably more successful in Russia. One important advantage over its American model is that many films and songs are available free of charge. Copyright complaints have had little effect on the business, as Russian courts have judged that the platform is not responsible for what its users upload.

On the wall of a house there's a billboard with the words: Alrosa for "United Russia"! Russia's largest diamond prospector, which has its headquarters here and is by far the biggest local employer, recommends voting for the party true to Putin. Alrosa is to Mirny what GM was to Detroit. The entire town of 37,000 only exists because sixty years ago geologists discovered a kimberlite pipe, which turned out to be very productive. A larger-than-life statue south of the city center depicts a local reindeer breeder and two scientists; the breeder was the one who led the scientists to the right spot all those years ago.

Today, Alrosa has a 25 percent share of the world diamond market and has broadened its business to other areas.

"There are rumors that the business is in the middle of a crisis and will soon no longer have funds to spend on airplanes, farming, and culture," says Marina. "Then it will concentrate on its core business of diamonds. That would be bad for me; my department would have less money for cultural events." Marina organizes concerts, theater performances, and occasional sporting events for young people. We stop in front of the building of a sports club. "Want to have a look inside?" Of course I do.

The receptionist, a fiftyish woman, is less enthusiastic about the idea. "This is a school, not a museum," she lectures us in a tone as cold as a January day in Sakha. Marina turns on all her charm, saying that she should make an exception for a German tourist. Well, okay, just down the hall and back, says the ice dragon.

At the end of the hall there is a basketball court. Pictures of soldiers at drill and heroes of World War II are hanging on the wall to provide motivation for peak performance. There's also a well-equipped boxing facility, a room for practicing gymnastics, and a fitness center with weights and other bodybuilding equipment. I hear the clicking of footsteps on linoleum coming toward us. The receptionist. Is she coming to kick us out because we've been wandering around for more than sixty seconds? Far from it. "Do you want to see the table tennis room? I'll turn on the light," she offers, unlocking a door. Marina winks at me and we inspect two modern table tennis tables. Finally we're allowed to look at a screen with black-and-white images from the surveillance cameras. Proudly, the receptionist points out the live images of a volleyball court, the hall on the upper floor, a wrestling hall and the forecourt. We thank her like well-behaved children and return to the street.

Truth No. 19:
Charm helps. Even on Russian gatekeepers.

DON'T WASTE
THE HEATING, PLEASE

ONE GENERAL STORE is called *Klondaik*; a restaurant, *Geofisik*; the cultural center, *Almas*, which means "diamond." I ask Marina whether you can buy precious stones here cheaper than elsewhere. "No. But you can get a bit of a diamond about the size of a speck of dust for 1,000 rubles."

There are rumors that black-market goods are smuggled off the company premises, despite stringent controls.

The residential buildings in Mirny are mainly eight- or nine-story, U-shaped, purpose-built structures on stilts, with parks and adventure playgrounds in the enclosed areas. Nothing in the city seems to be more modern than the castles and pirate ships for the little ones. It looks like they used all the paint for brightening up the playgrounds so there was none left for the house walls.

Signs point out that doors should always be closed to preserve heat. To get into a house you always have to pass through two, three, or four of them, so that in winter the cold remains outside. A gentleman would be confronted with an unsolvable problem if he wanted to open all the doors for a lady.

"You're lucky to be here now," says Marina. "Next week it's already going to be minus five." Today, however, she can still wear jeans with gaping holes without freezing.

The fur store is hidden right at the end of the top floor of the Mega Shopping Mall. Hundreds of velvet-soft black and white mink coats are hanging in an area of under thirteen square feet. None of them is cheaper than 120,000 rubles— around US$2,000—and many cost twice that amount. Who needs a secondhand car when you can buy such a status symbol? A cardboard sign points out that if fur becomes wet it should be well shaken before it's hung to improve its lifespan. Next to it, the name of the maker: EvropaGoldFur. This is odd as mink coats haven't really been fashionable in Europe for decades, and even inherited ones are nothing but trouble (Throw away? The poor animal. Wear? Not politically correct. Sell? Tricky). Maybe someone ought to organize an old mink collection and send the things back to Siberia.

"The winters really are a bit extreme here," says Marina. "But in recent years they've become warmer, often only minus thirty instead of minus forty."

"Then you're happy about climate change?" I ask.

"Oh, Jesus! No! We walk around on permafrost ground. If it gets too warm this will all be a lake. Do you want to see a polling station?"

From the square with the slightly wrong Lenin statue we go into the Almas Cultural Center. The entrance hall smells of popcorn; there's also a movie theater in the complex, which at

239

the moment is showing *Jason Bourne, Deepwater Horizon,* and the remake of *The Magnificent Seven.*

A B C

Walruses • МОРЖИ

The term given to intrepid heroes who go swimming in icy waters in the Russian winter. Orthodox Christians prefer doing this on January 19 because priests bless the waters and bathers can shock-freeze their sins. People who think that *morzhi* sounds like a quick sneeze are on the wrong track. According to popular belief, if you dip your head underwater three times during the winter plunge, you're sure to be free of colds for the rest of the year.

An arrow points to the polling station on the right, where wooden tables and pairs of women await citizens, who have to first register alphabetically. Four supervisors, wearing campaign buttons of different parties, sit next to the polling booths, which are behind curtains. The young man from United Russia is the most noticeable, with a red-and-white-striped tie, an undercut, and an expensive suit. Next to him is someone from the Communist Party of the Russian Federation, dressed in a shirt and jeans, and someone from A Just Russia, dressed similarly. And at the end of the row is Juliya, the business relations consultant of the city administration who was also one of my welcoming committee at the airport. "We are counting how many people voted," she explains. "But we are not allowed to speak to them; no one should be influenced." She has to be here from eight in the morning until eight at night. I wonder whether the voters really do feel unaffected with the three party representatives sitting there. If I had no idea who to vote for, I would probably look to see who was wearing the best tie or who looked the nicest.

Marina betrays whom she voted for a short while later in a small *shashlik* restaurant. On the wall is a clock with a Putin motif and she has great fun posing beneath it with thumbs up for a photo. Nevertheless she rails against the government readily and often. "For them the best people are the ones who just sit in front of the TV and are then frightened to leave their houses or cities, and as a result only learn about the world through the media," she says. There are probably more of them in an isolated outpost like Mirny than elsewhere. Is that why the most frightened people and the proudest nationalists often live in the sticks?

Back on the street we experience something like a scene from a dystopian apocalyptic movie. A black van with tinted windows and a loudspeaker on the roof drives slowly down the road. The same announcement is repeated over and over again: "Only one more hour. Make the right decision. Your life depends on how you vote today."

It turns out later that the 48 percent turnout in Sakha is almost exactly average for Russia. (However, the winners of the election, United Russia, got fewer votes here than in other regions. Maybe the loud tie made less of an impression than expected.)

We keep walking through Lenin Square and finally I realize 241 what's been bothering me about Lenin: he is sitting. As if the über-revolutionary was so confused by this place that he was forced to sit down. In all other cities I've visited he is always depicted standing, with a variety of gestures—enough to fill a self-help book on body language for managers and state leaders. The Mirny statue wouldn't make it into the book; here he sits lost in his thoughts, left forearm resting on his knee and slightly bewildered facial expression. The leader as thinker, with shoulders sagging; the pose has nothing dominant, nothing authoritative about it. The longer I look at him, the more he looks like someone hunched on his polished pedestal, asking the question: *Is this really what I wanted?*

Marina sometimes asks herself the same question. She dreams of getting away from Mirny. To Moscow or Saint Petersburg. Her parents are against it, though. "They say, 'You've got all you need here.'" She has been to England once, for two months, to take a language course. She liked it there; liked how the people interacted positively. "Russians are always very serious, weighed down by something, maybe money problems or bad business deals. Europeans seem happier," she says. "Since returning from England I laugh a lot more; some people think I'm crazy. How are the Germans?"

"Not really famous for their cheerful nature," I reply. "People complain a lot, especially about the weather."

"Oh, that's also a national pastime here, especially in winter."

"But I believe deep down inside that Germans get a sense of pleasure when they can complain about something. I grumble, therefore I am."

"I think our countries have a lot in common. Have I already told you that I learned German at school?"

"No."

"We mostly sang songs: 'Die Biene Maja,' 'Mein Hut, der hat drei Ecken,' 'Deutschland, Deutschland über alles,' such songs."

"Interesting mixture."

We say goodbye in front of a hospital with a larger-than-life mural of Yuri Gagarin. "We'll pick you up at home in two hours and then we'll party," she promises.

"Home" for me is an extended two-story wooden house, a residential facility primarily for teachers, who can live there rent-free. Room 11 is free at the moment because one of Marina's friends has just married and moved in with her husband. Inside it's extremely hot, although the heating device isn't on; there seems to be some sort of additional central heating. In winter it's probably a good thing, but now I have to open the window to avoid sweating.

A number of heavy jackets are hanging on a clothes rail, but no furs; the owner had probably taken them with her. Bookshelf—negative. A matryoshka doll of Obama, which, of course, out of curiosity I have to open. Inside it there is George W. Bush, then Bill Clinton, George Bush senior, and a tiny little Ronald Reagan. All the hated leaders of the traditional archenemy, so arranged that the successor contains his predecessor.

At the end of the corridor there is a washroom, shower, and communal kitchen. Teachers here seem to live a simpler life than people working for Alrosa or the municipality. As part of their salary they even get a kind of hardship bonus because of the living conditions in Mirny. Marina has sixty-five vacation days a year, plus nine official non-business days, and every two years her employer pays for a free holiday flight.

A B C

XB

At Easter, cakes and eggs are decorated with these Cyrillic letters. XB stands for *Kristos voskres*—"Christ is risen." A particularly tasty specialty is the *kulich*, a sweet cake made with raisins, vanilla, and cardamom, which also bears the symbol XB. They can even tell you about the future. If the crust doesn't crumble and the dough is well baked, you will have a good year.

I hear a song I recognize coming up from the street—"Brodyaga." "I'm penniless but have the most wonderful wife," and so on. The song was playing in the student's Lada on the trip from the airport to Mirny. At the same moment I get an unnecessary text: "We're waiting for you at the front door." I go down and climb into the car with Marina, Juliya, and the student, whose name is Igor and who is once more in the mood for dancing. My greeting committee from the first day is complete. It's astonishing how quickly after arriving at a new destination you begin to feel like part of a clique.

Igor puts his foot down and turns up the music so loud I can feel the thousands of tiny hairs in my inner ear disappearing forever. "You should come here in winter, then I'll teach you all about drifting," screams Igor. What he means is death-defying spinning and sliding techniques when driving on ice.

The Globe is hidden in a nondescript industrial building and has two rooms, one for eating, drinking, and talking and the other for eating, drinking, and dancing. We start off the evening in the talking room with an electric shisha that was supposed to be orange-flavored but tastes like citrus bathroom cleaner. To make up for it, the water container has a purple glow.

More and more beautiful women, dressed to impress, flood in amid clouds of perfume, and we talk about the worldwide number-one nightclub topic: the search for a partner.

Marina: Her parents want her to marry as soon as possible, at the very latest at twenty-five. They want to have grandchildren; preferably their son-in-law should be from Azerbaijan or Georgia, and he should definitely be a Muslim.

Igor: His parents want him to marry a Russian and his friends agree. By Russian they mean Slavonic, so no one from Sakha and not a Muslim. He knows many young athletes and they all have problems on the marriage market. "They don't smoke, don't drink, don't party. This apparently makes them boring," says the twenty-year-old. "But when they move to other cities they quickly find stunning girlfriends. A friend of mine has just married in Novosibirsk—a super girl, slim and domestic, and she makes the best pancakes." Igor is secretly in love with a woman named Lisa, but she is eight years older and completed her studies a while ago. "I'm a student, I have no money and no house. I have nothing to offer her," he says.

Juliya: Her parents have almost given up. She is slim, tall, and beautiful but at twenty-nine she already feels that the

245

choice in Mirny is limited, if she doesn't want someone too difficult or too young, as most people marry in their early twenties. She is out of the question for Igor's athlete friends as she comes from Sakha and has Asian facial features.

There must be a simpler way.

The traditional reindeer nomads in Sakha did things differently. When they met men from other regions, the outsiders were cordially invited to get the nomads' wives pregnant. In nomadic communities, almost everybody was related to one another, and they knew that different genetic material would guarantee healthier children.

After the theoretical part of the evening we're ready for the dance floor in the other room. Disco ball, brick walls, a brightly colored neon sign advertising cocktails. It smells of alcohol and garlic as here, too, hearty meals are served.

At the moment there are only women on the dance floor; the men need a few more drinks. Russian dance-pop seems to be the most popular genre; when Shakira or Beyoncé is played, the dancers return to their seats or to the bar.

All of a sudden it's break time for the guests when a strongly built man, light on his feet and with a proud swagger in his shoulders, showcases a Caucasian dance. Every step and every turn embodies an amount of anger and resolve that would intimidate even Maori haka dancers. Only his glassy eyes don't quite match the precision of his movements. Finally the man clenches a schnapps glass from the floor with his teeth and, without using his hands, knocks it back before tossing it behind him with a whiplash movement of his head. For the rest of the evening you can hear the sounds of glass shards being trodden on by high heels. "Not a marriage candidate," muses Marina, who herself is a fantastic dancer.

246

Another young gentleman, however, has caught her eye. "I'm a bit shy," she confesses. "But I don't think men want a woman who is too adventurous or crazy."

We don't arrive at a definite conclusion about what men or women want. Late at night, Igor drives us all home, but not before making a slight detour on a straight road to push his Lada to its limits. With music, of course. *I'm a poor tramp, but I will marry the most wonderful woman in the world.*

The next day I revisit the diamond mine. It's a forty-five-minute walk down dusty streets between the modern factory buildings of an old industry. Young truck drivers transport earth from the mine in numbered yellow dump trucks from the Belarusian company BelAZ. Surface mining has been phased out, but Alrosa continues its underground mining operations for precious stones, and a lot of debris accumulates. A couple of tons of waste material for a few carats of diamonds. But business is good: in the forty-four years before the closure of the Mir mine, almost US$19 billion worth of diamonds was extracted.

A wedding party in expensive SUVs drive past honking, which sounds like muffled ship's horns. There's no security fence or guards around the perimeter of the crater, just plenty of danger signs with lots of exclamation marks. People who are tired of life and wish to go climbing here have no other obstacles to overcome.

A better recommendation for climbing can be found on a nearby hill, on top of which a huge crane and dumpster have been placed as a monument. A couple of kids are doing gymnastics on the scoop and loading platform.

The view of the airport is spectacular from here. Through the mist you can see huge scrapped Tupolev phantom planes. Pilots have to observe special regulations here—no helicopters or planes are allowed to fly above the mine because of the treacherous downwashes. In winter, before takeoff and landing, the runway has to be leveled to make it useable.

I get into a conversation with Olga and Dmitri. He's in the ninth grade, she's one class below. "We're glad to meet a foreigner because we can practice our English on you," says Dmitri. "Now we've got a story to tell our teacher. Normally you never see tourists here."

The Muscovite architect Nikolay Lyutomsky would love to change that. Under the banner "Eco City 2020" he presents his bold concept of transforming the huge hole into a multistory ecological city, with gardens and natural ventilation, a glass dome, and solar cells that will provide enough energy for the 100,000 inhabitants. If this dream were to become reality, tourists would be sure to come. But for now it's pure fiction, though one illustrated with some fine sketches.

I think that the open mine in its present state is much more interesting. A void created by decades of donkeywork. A void as a warning of what human greed can do to the landscape. A void with a visitor's terrace.

★

SUPERJET TO
KHABAROVSK

THE BAGGAGE DROP-OFF at Mirny airport is a storage room. There are no conveyor belts; I just pass it on through an iron door. Will I ever see my backpack again?

The plane, however, soon relativizes my concerns about my dirty laundry and second pair of shoes. It's a Sukhoi Superjet 100, the latest achievement of Russian engineering skills. Its commercial launch didn't run all that smoothly, though. Four years ago in Indonesia a Superjet 100 crashed on a demonstration flight for journalists and potential customers, killing everyone on board. Since then, seventy-one machines have been delivered, most of them flying in Russia, a few in Mexico, and none in Indonesia.

Up until then I had been surprised that I hadn't flown in a Russian machine. One stage of the journey I took a Ukrainian Antonov; other than that they were always Bombardiers or Airbuses. The notoriously noisy Tupolevs and Yakovlevs from

Soviet times are becoming rare. Sky travelers are still not encouraged to have too much fun—entertainment screens on every seat are not to be expected in Russia.

As far as airlines go, I have learned to appreciate Aeroflot. Not only because of the sensationally fashionable uniforms of the stewardesses, but because the machines are comparatively punctual, look fairly modern, and are not regularly falling from the sky anymore, as they did in the '70s and '80s. Not long ago, I used to avoid Russian airlines when flying to Asia, even if the competitor cost a bit more. On this trip, I'm happy when I can take an Aeroflot plane for domestic flights. But they don't fly to Mirny, so I'm now traveling with Yakutia Airlines, a small company with just thirteen planes. The smaller companies are the worst. According to statistics from 2015, the risk of an accident on internal Russian flights is four times the global average. This is probably why passengers still clap after every landing here.

An unobservant passenger would hardly notice the difference between a Superjet and a Boeing or an Airbus. The cabin seems to tend a bit more toward plastic; the sound of the motors is a bit more like an electric razor. But the whole design, even the overhead reading lights and the ventilation fans, are similar in style and emit similar chemical smells.

Just as I sit down at seat 14A, the motor chokes. There could be a variety of reasons for this. Ten minutes later the pilot restarts and taxies to the runway.

The Sukhoi Superjet lifts off and stays in the air for the planned amount of time. The engines don't drop into the taiga and the oxygen masks remain in the overhead paneling, although there is quite a bit of turbulence before the landing. When we arrive in Khabarovsk, the pilot thoroughly deserves the applause.

Truth No. 20:

The vast majority of passengers and crew members on internal Russian flights reach their destination alive.

★

HONEST ALCOHOL

A PROFESSIONALLY INDUCED VODKA intoxication differs from other intoxications in that there are long-lasting moments of unusual clarity. It lacks the dullness of beer drunkenness, the dizziness of whiskey, the excitability of Cuba Libre, or the knockout effect of randomly drinking everything possible.

The "most honest of all drinks" is how Russians describe their favorite spirit, because it has no taste and has never been romanticized like whiskey or wine. There is no excuse to consume it other than wanting to get drunk. As an experiment, U.S. researchers served study participants either whiskey or vodka until they reached a blood alcohol level of 0.11 percent (I would love to have seen the "Test subjects wanted" ad in the newspaper). The next day the whiskey drinkers not only felt worse than the vodka drinkers, but they were not as good at solving concentration problems. The West vs. Russia, 0:1.

What would the findings have been if the participants had obeyed not only rule number one of Russian drinking pros (no mixing), but also rule number two? This stipulates a strict intake of food while boozing. Grandma's porcini mushrooms doused in sunflower oil, cold smoked pike, boiled potatoes with dill, caviar. Some people swear by mini rituals that are "dead certain" to prevent a hangover the next day—sniff a piece of rye bread, exhale heavily, drink, then eat the bread, or eat a third of a pickled gherkin before drinking and the rest afterward.

I experiment with different variations on the formula but don't reach an empirically clear-cut conclusion. What else happened in Khabarovsk, who my host was, and what I was actually doing there I have forgotten, which is pretty strange as in between I had a number of moments of clarity.

The next thing I remember is that after three days someone with a large Jeep brings me to the main station and directs me to a train to Vladivostok.

A B C
Yandex • ЯНДЕКС

Name of the first internet search engine to offer services in Cyrillic, beginning in 1997 With 57 percent of the market today, the company still has a greater proportion than Google (35 percent), even though the American company has recently been gaining on it. Both business models are similar: Yandex also offers maps, advertising, translations, an email program, and a browser. Its cab app is very successful; with it you can often get from A to B in Russian cities much more cheaply than if you deal directly with cab drivers.

RESHUFFLING
THE CARDS

IN THE MONTHS before and after my travels in Russia quite a lot has happened on the political front. The British voted for Brexit in a referendum. Donald Trump was elected president of the U.S. He began treating European allies like enemies, creating a divide between Western countries. Two other changes received hardly any attention in international news: Igor Dodon became the new president of Moldavia and Rumen Radev the new president of Bulgaria, which took over presidency of the Council of the European Union on January 1, 2018.

The news has a noteworthy common thread—everything has happened exactly as Russia would have wished. If world politics were a sporting event, you would have to say that Putin is the athlete of the moment, as all the abovementioned politicians are, compared to their predecessors or competitors, on a Russia-friendly course.

And then there is Aleppo. Syria's President Assad and his Russian and Iranian allies have managed to regain control of the city from the rebels. Both sides have been accused of violations of the laws of armed conflict. Up to now Russia has succeeded in fending off the most severe accusations, even though Amnesty International has provided credible evidence of many civilian deaths from Russian air strikes.

The situation in Syria has strengthened Putin's military position. And it has gained him much respect—even Barack Obama, a declared opponent of Putin, classified Russia as a "military superpower," which, behind the scorn, was received in Russia with hidden pride.

Donald Trump's election victory was greeted with spontaneous applause in the national Duma parliament; possibly the jubilation had to do equally with the defeat of the much-hated Hillary Clinton. Even if a bare-chested Trump doesn't ride off into the sunset with Putin, as depicted in online photo montages, Russia can only win with this president. As far as foreign policies are concerned, Trump acts impulsively and not ideologically, is less insistent about "Western values" than his predecessor, and is open to making deals with leaders who, although not big fans of human rights, are nice to him. Russian propaganda always presented the U.S. and the whole "West"

255

as hypocritical and manipulative, and now the most powerful man in the world is a perfect and obvious example for that. The current U.S. president comes across as a dubious dictator, making the Russian president seem like a beacon of reliability and clarity. From interviews, it is obvious which of the two is intellectually superior. It was clearly not a good idea to arrange a meeting between them with no advisers present, as happened in July of 2018—the result being a historic disaster for American diplomacy.

There's another thread in the abovementioned news. In each case there has been evidence that Russian manipulation played a role in shaping outcomes, either through propaganda, hacking, internet trolls, or all of them together. Whether the results were really influenced in every case is hard to say, but it is possible.

No world leader knows more about the workings of the security service than ex-KGB man Putin. A number of years ago he began devoting a significant part of the military budget to information warfare, and it's possible this is now proving to be a stroke of genius. Who needs to deploy old-fashioned soldiers and initiate regime change operations with its secret service when it's much cheaper and simpler to influence opinions on elections in other countries?

RT claims they just try to popularize their own culture and points of view abroad, like Voice of America, Deutsche Welle, or the Chinese CCTV International. But the Russians do it far more aggressively and steadfastly. And they reflect the zeitgeist—the discussions about fake news and a post-fact society ironically play right into the hands of those who have broadcast long and loud to trust no one.

During the U.S. election the Clinton camp sometimes

played the old Russia-is-to-blame card a bit too readily. Familiar bogeyman, easy to explain, an ever-welcome excuse.

But since then even Trump has admitted that Russian hackers with links to the government sabotaged the Clinton campaign by, for instance, accessing the emails of her campaign chairman, John Podesta. Such an intrusion in a foreign country's election is a success in a métier in which the U.S. has been the world leader for decades.

It's interesting how Russia is on everyone's lips again. If world-power status can be measured by how often your country appears on the news, then Putin is on the right path. And when fears in the West are stoked a bit more than is actually necessary, from a Russian standpoint there's no harm done; this merely allows Russia to appear more powerful than it really is. In the world of attention, the same rules apply to politics as to rock stars who manage to come up with a new scandal every week. Putin knows this, and he's learned a lot since stepping into office for the first time.

Every other national leader probably would have rejected accusations of influencing the U.S. election in a matter-of-fact, diplomatic manner. Putin, in contrast, didn't repudiate the claims but countered with a rhetorical question: "Is the U.S a banana republic? America is a superpower. Correct me if I'm wrong."

In career advice books you sometimes read that people who want to get to the top should begin by dressing and acting like their superiors; this increases their chances of reaching the boardroom. Other criteria, such as their aptitude, their actual power, or the objective quality of their work are then no longer so decisive, as all their colleagues will see that this person has the right stuff to be a leader.

The same principle works in world politics. A small test of how much resonance state propaganda can have in one's own country is to ask a Russian which country has a similar GDP to theirs. The correct answer usually results in disbelief. The countries near Russia in the global rankings are South Korea, Australia, Canada, and Mexico. But what role do South Korea or Mexico have in geopolitical questions or in influencing international opinion?

Is anyone still surprised that Putin has given his countrymen back their pride?

SAME FACTS,
DIFFERENT OUTCOMES

"**O**F **COURSE THE** Russian TV shows propaganda," says Yuri from Vladivostok. "The foreign media does exactly the same. But I'm convinced that our propaganda is good for the country."

We're sitting in a small one-room apartment in the north of the city. The tiny kitchen is in the hall, between sea-blue walls with golden stars. A mountain bike, which is more expensive than all the furniture, rests against the windowsill in the living room. Yuri is fifty-seven and works as in marine research for a state-run institute associated with the Ministry of Fisheries. There he leads a team of twenty people whose main task is to monitor fish stocks and analyze any irregularities.

"Which propaganda is good for Russia?" I ask.

"The media mostly stresses one central idea: people's living standards should improve."

"And are they?"

"In the last fifteen years much has changed for the better. I'm not a fan of Putin but I see no one with a better vision for the country."

He goes to the kitchen and returns with two mugs of tea.

"But didn't things deteriorate for people after the Crimean crisis? And still Putin's approval ratings rocketed afterward."

"I admit, since then things have not gotten better. But they haven't gotten worse. I think 80 percent of people here don't notice the sanctions in their everyday lives."

Five minutes later he tells me that at the moment there's nothing that would induce him to sell the empty apartment in which we're now sitting, because the ruble is so low. Well then, some things have gotten worse in recent years.

"How can you be so sure that the government means well with the propaganda? Would it not make more sense for them to focus on their own interests and gains in power?"

"That depends on the government. If the government's actions are good for people then their propaganda is also good for people."

Yuri is an alert guy, a highly educated scientist, someone who in his professional life is always searching for data that can be substantiated. I'm a bit bewildered by his good faith, which reminds me of the Vissarion followers in Siberia. I can sense that he's not an out-and-out Putin admirer, but that he's just pragmatic.

But maybe the explanation is not that complicated. He was born in 1959 and in his whole life he has never experienced an independent news media. Isn't it then quite logical to differentiate between mendacious and slightly less mendacious propaganda? The desire to subordinate to a strong leader who is felt to be just seems to be much stronger in Russia than in the West.

been shaded in the national colors—red, blue, and white. So far, quite the status symbol.

What's puzzling, however, is where it leads: to an island of the same name, about the size of Manhattan but with a population of only a few thousand, some pretty hiking trails on the coast, and plenty of nature. Once Russky was a restricted military zone, and you can still find the ruins of watchtowers, forts, and depots there. In the summer it's a popular place for mushroom hunting.

Okay, so there is a modern university (which is where the APEC summit was held), an aquatic complex, and a brand-new oceanarium, but nothing that would justify an infrastructure project of this size; the huge bridge could hardly be described as busy. It's almost as if Switzerland had built the Gotthard Base Tunnel just to provide an improved link to a small but attractive skiing area in a remote valley that up until then had been inaccessible.

The idea was to establish a first-class tourist destination on Russky Island. Thanks, for instance, to the drawing power of the oceanarium, a futuristic building with a roof in the shape of a gigantic shell, located right on the shores of the Sea of Japan. It has just opened after a four-year delay; many things didn't go according to plan—they accidentally forgot to build a visitors' parking lot, and even before the first ticket was sold, so many animals had died under mysterious circumstances (including two walruses named Fanya and Mira, a bottlenose dolphin named Leo, and three beluga whales) that it won't be long before Greenpeace gets wind and starts making a fuss. But the bridge is solid enough.

"I do compare to other media sources," he says. "I receive BBC, Fox News, Belarusian, Ukrainian, and even Vietnamese channels. Every morning at breakfast I watch Euronews."

"And what are the differences to Russian channels?"

"Generally you have the same basic facts. The ranking and the additional information are different."

"Can you give me an example?"

"Today it was about the bombing of an aid convoy in Syria. It was broadcast everywhere, none of them ignored it. Euronews added that American sources suspected Russia was behind the airstrike. Channel One also mentioned that, but added that Russian officials had denied responsibility."

"What do you think about talk shows? Sometimes there's the impression that people with anti-Russian viewpoints are only invited so they can be shouted down."

"There are different shows, I prefer watching the STS channel. But I have my doubts about whether foreign politicians are real or actors. For years I've been seeing the same faces of apparently Ukrainian politicians. They must live permanently in Moscow; how can they do politics from there?"

A short while later he thanks me for the talk and says goodbye as he has to get back to his wife. Once again I have an apartment all to myself.

IN THE MIDDLE of Vladivostok there is a huge plastic goalpost with the word *Finish* emblazoned on the crossbar. Hundreds of spectators are there; in the Square of Fighters for the Revolution, a stage has been erected for dance performances, and Svetlanskaya Street has been cordoned off. TV crews are out and about; someone is making excited loudspeaker announcements; excessively beautiful cheerleaders are waving pom-poms.

It really wasn't really necessary to make such a fuss about my arrival at my final destination, but still, it's a nice gesture. Although I'm not quite sure why there are so many sweaty people wandering around with numbers and "Vladivostok International Marathon" printed on their T-shirts.

I climb over the barriers, run across the finish line, and quickly disappear toward the Tokyo Sushi Bar. Vladivostok has many Japanese and Chinese restaurants offering authentic nigiri, jiaozi dumplings, and kung pao chicken. There's even a North Korean restaurant called Pyongyang. The waitresses wear snappy uniforms, and every evening at the stroke of eight, they perform a couple of karaoke songs oozing with corniness (the duck with paprika also oozes, but with fat).

It's only eighty miles from here to the Friendship Bridge at the border to North Korea; China is even nearer, and the *Eastern Dream* ferry takes passengers to South Korea and on to Japan.

Most of the cars in the city are right-hand drive because of the massive amounts of secondhand Toyotas and Hondas that were imported, at least until 2009, when the government in Moscow began slapping a hefty tax on Japanese cars. Many small importers had to give up their businesses; there were angry demonstrations, but they had no effect.

Vladivostok, seven time zones away from Moscow and lying on the hills at the head of Golden Horn Bay, seems as if someone has flung some Far Eastern and Russian culture into a blender and pressed the button; the resulting mixture turns out to be one of the few attractive cities in the country. Stylish pubs and baroque cafés line the side streets; young couples stroll along the crumbling promenade.

A B C

Zapoy • ЗАПОЙ

One of the many Russian words relating to alcohol for which there is no corresponding term in other languages. It describes a person who spends a number of days in continuous drunkenness. The terms *suchnyak* and *nedoperepil* are thematically related. The former describes the rough feeling in the throat after a boozy night. The latter refers to someone who is certainly drunker than is good for him, but not as drunk as he theoretically could be.

The 750-foot reinforced concrete pylons of the Zolotoy Bridge, opened in 2012, look like giant chopsticks. Thanks to them, the cityscape now looks a little bit like San Francisco. The Russky Bridge, a few miles to the south, is even more impressive, its central span distance making it the world's longest cable-stayed bridge. It was constructed in preparation for the Asia-Pacific Economic Cooperation (APEC) summit in 2012, using the latest anti-earthquake and anti-storm technology, and cost an estimated US$1.1 billion. Its steel cables have

UNDERPANTS AND
TINFOIL HATS

THE LAST HOST on my travels is named Nikita and hardly speaks a word to me. To balance things out, though, he has a roommate named Igor who talks absolutely too much. I had to change hosts as Yuri, the marine biologist, had already planned to have two other guests for the weekend.

The kitchen and bathroom of the apartment on Tiger Street look as though no new piece of equipment or furniture has been acquired in the last forty years. Had they been better preserved, the washing machine and fridge would make great exhibits in a design museum. The light switch in the kitchen consists of two wires that have to be connected. This is particularly important at night so as not to entangle your head, because the only way to move around is by ducking under the washing lines running from the dining table to the sink. The apartment smells of cheap men's deodorant, wet laundry, and old chicken meat.

The living room serves as a bedroom. Nikita spends most of his time sprawled out on his double-bed mattress, which, due to the lack of a bed, is on the floor. Igor has the opposite corner, right next to the door to the balcony; a small pillow with a bear pattern on it and a woolen blanket are enough for him, and he sleeps directly on the carpet. The five loudspeakers with the brand names *Dialog* and *Genius*, which form a small wall on one side of his "bed," seem to be more important for his comfort. An Asus Nexus tablet serves as his link to human knowledge, to the latest Ultimate Spiderman series, and to the hip-hop songs of Oxxxymiron and Loc-Dog. Six square feet of your own world.

Reticence and talkativeness are not their only opposite qualities. Nikita has a lot of hair, Igor none. Nikita wears track pants at home, Igor underpants. Nikita reads books, Igor the internet. Nikita sleeps a lot, Igor is awake a lot.

On the first evening Igor and I talk about Russia and the world. Igor thinks President Putin is a criminal. For one reason: because of the bomb attack in Moscow shortly before his inauguration, for which Chechen terrorists were blamed. "There was a journalistic investigation and according to this it was the FSB who were behind it." Indeed, the case hasn't been solved yet, and some evidence supports this version of events. A number of investigators carrying out research have been killed; the most famous of them, ex-FSB agent Alexander Litvinenko, died of polonium poisoning. "At that time Yeltsin had to boost his popularity ratings. Nobody knew Putin when he was named as successor. The bombing attack gave them an opportunity to strike against Chechnya; they needed a successful war. For every leader it's the best way to increase popularity."

On the second evening the conversation becomes awkward.

Igor tries to convince me that there were far fewer deaths during the Holocaust than most people believe. His source of information: an online report of a farmer who had delivered food to Auschwitz and spoke of the relatively civilized conditions. In addition to this, Igor claims that the number who apparently died actually outnumbered the worldwide population of Jews at that time. "You can google it," he says.

My remarks that you can also google that Hitler is still living in Argentina, that UFOs land every day, and that governments poison their own subjects with gas don't seem to impress him. The more I listen to him, the more our discussion gets out of control, the more probable it seems that maybe he really does google all of that stuff from time to time.

He thinks that from birth whites are superior to blacks and believes all of Africa to be a realm of chaos in which only "savages" live. You can read about it on the internet and a friend of a friend of a friend has been there. I tell him of my own travels to Ghana, where at no time was I surrounded by half-naked warriors dancing and waving spears. It doesn't seem to challenge his views. "That was a British colony. Everything that's civilized there came from the whites."

So much for Africa; now onto Europe and the refugee crisis. "You're too liberal, too tolerant," says Igor. "I've read that in London the most common name for newborn babies is Mohammed. In twenty years England will be a caliphate."

Russia is not suitable for refugees from Arabic countries, according to Igor. "Here you have to work really hard, it's not as easy to get benefits as it is in your country." Later, however, he admits that he couldn't imagine working five days a week; it would be "slavery." He only works on Wednesdays and Saturdays in the depot of a large distribution company that specializes in flowers. As his rent is low, he has enough to live on.

We discuss the CIA and the Rockefellers; he praises the scientific achievements of the Nazis regarding ethnology and criticizes the European "programming" which considers all people to be equal. He also rails against the dangers in the "black hoods" of New York, although in all his life he has never been outside Russia.

He ignores counterarguments that don't fit his views of the world. Either the authorities have "hushed something up" or something has been proven because it corresponds to his sense of truth, and on top of this there are google hits. "Unfortunately many people are easy to manipulate," says Igor, and that may be the truest statement he has made in three days.

Truth No. 21:
People should travel more instead of sitting in front of a computer.

The reality outside the apartment is considerably more pleasing than what Igor thinks is reality, so I decide to make a trip to Russky Island. The 15 bus takes me across the huge bridge; the 29 bus gets me into the wilds. A small parking lot, a gravel path, and then thick forest. Suddenly a fox emerges from the undergrowth and blocks my path. As I have no snacks to offer him, he soon continues on his way.

Russky: it sounds a little like a smaller version of Russia. Maybe the island epitomizes the whole. Forbidding cliffs on the outside, lush forests on the inside. Much untamed nature, low population density, a few hidden military bunkers that you can only recognize if you look really hard. A place searching for new perspectives; to be precise, Russky is gambling on education (the university) and tourism (the bridge and the oceanarium). The concept is not all that clear. Maybe there is no concept.

Once you're out of the forest, small paths lead along the spectacular coastal cliffs. One false step and you fall into the abyss. I mull over Igor and his perspective of the world, about "savages" in Africa and all the conspiracy theories. There are a number of mistakes that he makes in his online searches for information, but to me one of the most basic ones is that he holds extremes to be the truth and anything normal to be the exception.

At least this is not uncommon. To varying degrees, everybody has preconceptions of other countries because the information we receive on top of what we know already mostly concerns the extraordinary and not the ordinary. Time and again when I arrive at an airport in a new country I'm reminded of my own preconceptions and marvel about how modern everything is. This is because the majority of images I've viewed prior to the trip show the traditional aspects of culture and not the modern ones. Market traders, not managers; Ladas, not Toyotas; mountain villages, not shopping malls.

And Russia? Onion domes, matryoshka dolls, balalaikas, and prefabs? There are all of those and much more. Russia includes so many microcosms and microcultures that you feel as if you've traveled around the globe without ever having left the country. Behind the gruff exterior beats a huge heart. And behind the hostility that some people seem to feel toward the West, there lies a sense of disappointment with the West. Or the idea that the West hates Russia, proof of which is shown every evening on TV. I didn't bring any hatred with me and in return experienced no ill will. On my travels I got to know at least ninety-nine wonderful people and just one idiot. It certainly wasn't a representative selection. People offering accommodation to foreign guests belong in all probability to the more likable representatives of their country.

Do I now plan on buying a T-shirt with "I Love Putin" on it? No. But I do understand what makes Putin's country tick and what his popularity means. And I've witnessed how state media can influence the way people think.

I hope that one day soon a Russian journalist will take three months to couchsurf throughout Europe and write a book about his or her experiences. From the Baltic States to Greece, from Spain to Denmark; I'm convinced that a different image of Europe would emerge from that presented every day on Channel One or RT. In Hamburg, of course, there is a couch waiting in my apartment with full board. And once their book is finished, we could go together on a lecture tour from Málaga to Kamchatka.

270   The island path on Russky goes over gray crags down to the sea all the way out to the tip of Cape Tobizina. Families spread their picnic blankets; a rotund man bears his naked belly to the sun; dogs scamper around. My travels end on the shores of the

Sea of Japan, almost six thousand miles east of Moscow and still in the same country.

"From Germany? All alone? Aren't you frightened?" a cheerful old hiker with a lavish mustache and more gaps in his teeth than teeth asks me.

"If we were all a little less fearful, we would achieve a great deal," I reply without thinking. I surprise myself with this piece of fortune-cookie wisdom. Then I pull off my boots, roll up my pants, and take a few steps into the water. It's not as cold as I expected.

★

ACKNOWLEDGMENTS

I WOULD CORDIALLY LIKE to thank a number of people and creatures; without their inspiration, support, and general greatness this book wouldn't have been possible. The couch-surfers: Nadya in Novosibirsk, Genrich in Moscow, Vladimir in Moscow, Murad and Ruslan in Grozny, Renat in Makhach-kala, Vladimir in Makhachkala, Altana in Elista, Alexei in Astrakhan, Krisia and Sergei in Volgograd, Yuri the cab driver, Alexander in Simferopol, Alisa and Konstantin in Bakhchysarai, Sasha in Sevastopol, Arina in Saint Petersburg, Sveta in Saint Petersburg, Anna in Saint Petersburg, Victoria in Saint Peters-burg, Teena and Gleb in Yekaterinburg, Olga in Yekaterinburg, Yevgeni in Novosibirsk, Irina in Ust-Koksa, Chalka in Edigan, Vitalia in Krasnoyarsk, Alex in Zharovsk, Minna in Zharovsk, Yevgeni in Kyzyl, Ayu in Kyzyl, Sergei in Khuzhir, Kirill and Anya and Wanya and Bella in Yakutsk, Marina and Juliya and Igor in Mirny, Yaroslav in Khabarovsk, Natalya in Khabarovsk, Yekaterina in Vladivostok, Yuri in Vladivostok, Nikita and Igor in Vladivostok. And the many other friendly people with whom I talked or who gave me tips or spontaneous Russian lessons on my travels.

Nora Reinhardt, Cathrin Klapp, Anastasiya Izhak, Rebeca Martínez Bermejo, Tonia Sorrentino, Gulliver Theis, Felicitas von Lovenberg, Bettina Feldweg, Verena Pritschov, Vladimir Sevrinovski, Janine Borse, Ben Wadewitz, Anton Krotov, Alexander Fedorov, Petra Eggers, Antje Blinda, Anja Tiedge, Verena Töpper, Stefan Schultz, Natascha Romanova, Mina Esfandiari, Juliya Samus, Alexandra Estrina, Petra Eggers, Florian Harms, Mira Brusch, Gilda Sahebi, Racquel and Nunu from the Casa Diversa on La Gomera, Gizmo the cat, Bernd Ruffer, Theresa Lachner, Hallie Gu, Christina Hebel, Paniz Gholinejad, Mayra Quintanar Helgueros, and Traudl and Uli, my parents.

The following institutions and people had no influence whatsoever on the contents of this book: the CIA, the FBI, Vladimir Putin, the FSB, Angela Merkel, Petro Poroshenko, Sergey Lavrov, Barack Obama, the Bilderberg Group, the World Anti-Doping Agency, and the Illuminati.

NOTES

1   Heine, Heinrich. "The Lorelei." English translation by A.Z. Foreman. *Poems in Translation* (blog). poemsintranslation.blogspot.ca/2009/11/heinrich-heine-lorelei-from-german.html.

2   The *"Domostroi": Rules for Russian Households in the Time of Ivan the Terrible.* Edited and translated by Carolyn Johnston Pouncy. Ithaca, NY: Cornell University Press, 1994.

3   Wikipedia (German), "Speisesalz." English translation by Jamie McIntosh. Retrieved from de.wikipedia.org/wiki/Speisesalz.

4   Moss, Walter G. *A History of Russia Volume I: To 1917.* London: Anthem Press, 2003, p. 18.

5   Gogol, Nikolai. "Nevski Prospect." *Diary of a Madman and Other Stories.* Edited by Mary Carolyn Waldrep and Thomas Crawford. Mineola, NY: Dover, 2006, p. 20. Translation adapted by Jamie McIntosh.

6   Gogol, Nikolai. "Nevsky Prospect." *The Collected Tales of Nikolai Gogol.* Translated by Richard Pevear and Larissa Volokhonsky. New York: Vintage Classics, 1999, p. 278.

7   Roerich, Nikolai. *Altai-Himalaya: A Travel Diary.* New York: Nicholas Roerich Museum, 2017. Retrieved from roerich.org/roerich-writings-altai-himalaya.php.

8   "The Soviet National Anthem." English translation from marxists.org/history/ussr/sounds/lyrics/anthem.htm.

9   Wikipedia, "National anthem of Russia." English translation from
    en.wikipedia.org/wiki/National_anthem_of_Russia.

10 Vissarion. *Das Letzte Testament*. English translation by Jamie McIntosh.
    Retrieved from vissarion.info/wadim101.htm.

11 Vissarion. *Book of Appeal*. Promised Land—Community of Vissarion web-
    site. Retrieved from vissarion.eu/en/Last%20Testament/Book%20of%20
    Appeal.htm.

12 Mühling, Jens. *A Journey into Russia*. London: Haus, 2015.

13 Tyutchev, Fyodor. "Russia cannot be understood with the mind alone."
    English translation from Wikiquote, "Fyodor Tyutchev." en.wikiquote.org/
    wiki/Fyodor_Tyutchev.